IMAGES OF ENGLAND

COAL MINERS OF
CANNOCK
CHASE

IMAGES OF ENGLAND

COAL MINERS OF
CANNOCK
CHASE

JUNE PICKERILL

TEMPUS

Frontispiece: The Valley Pit, Hednesford, now the site of the Museum of Cannock Chase. On the left side of the photograph in the distance is Bradbury Lane. The colliery was opened in 1874 and closed in 1962.

First published 2006

Tempus Publishing Limited
The Mill, Brimscombe Port,
Stroud, Gloucestershire, GL5 2QG
www.tempus-publishing.com

© June Pickerill, 2006

The right of June Pickerill to be identified as the Author
of this work has been asserted in accordance with the
Copyrights, Designs and Patents Act 1988.

British Library Cataloguing in Publication Data.
A catalogue record for this book is available from the British Library.

ISBN 0 7524 3815 8

Typesetting and origination by Tempus Publishing Limited.
Printed in Great Britain.

Contents

Acknowledgements

This book could not have been compiled without the help of the following contributors:

The late Mr R. Brookes, Mr E. Bailey, Mr Birch, Mrs J. Barnett, Mr and Mrs J. Crabtree, the late Mr Harry Edwards, Mr Edwards, Mrs S. Everitt, Mr R. Fullelove BEM, Mrs Sheila Green, Mr G. Harvey, Mrs Joyce Lane, Mr G. Lee, Mr Dick Mason, Mrs E. Martin, the late Mr Sam Morris, Mrs Joyce Pook, Mr Pockett, Mrs M. Powiss, Mr E. Rotchell, Mr Horace Spruce, Mr Cliff Schofield, Mr Barry Tatler, the late Mr Arthur Wilkes, Mr D. Williams, Mr Gordon Woodhead, Mrs E. Wright, Mrs Hannaford and Mr Wilf Nicholls who gave me permission to use his research into fatal accidents at the various collieries.

I apologise in advance if names are spelled incorrectly – they are as given to me by the owners of the photographs – and also if anyone by mistake has been left off the above list.

The photographs for the cover are reproduced by the kind permission of the Museum of Cannock Chase and the map on page 8 was loaned by the Cannock Chase Mining Historical Society.

The topics covered in this book have been reliant upon the material available, and any further unpublished photographs or documentation that readers might have in their possession, or further information on the subjects contained in the book, would be gratefully received.

Introduction

I was inspired to compile this volume of photographs by one that appeared in *Cannock Chase – The Second Selection*, which was published in 1997. I have been on a mission ever since to collect as many photographs as possible of miners and their workplaces, their families and their activities outside work. I realised back then how quickly we were losing not only the images but also the memories of a now defunct industry, and that this should not be allowed to happen.

As in any book of photographs, it is only as good as the material people are willing to lend, so some areas are not covered at all. Of course, many miners prior to nationalisation would not be able to afford a camera, so images taken at home or outside work are really precious. I have also been told many times, that miners were reluctant to be photographed because they thought 'it was sissy' – their words, not mine.

Mining was a huge local industry affecting most local people, but in compiling this book I realised how little I know about it, despite having lived in a mining community all my life, with both grandfathers working 'down the pit'.

I have not touched on the technical side of the industry – I leave that to others far more qualified to do so – but have concentrated on the personal lives of the miners as described to me, so any technical terms used are as provided by the owners of the photographs.

Outside their working hours, miners and their families were a dominant section of the community, always willing to play their part. As well as supporting the churches and chapels, Working Men's Clubs, and numerous societies, groups, associations and choirs, to name a few, they also raised money at the galas and carnivals to help the local hospitals, send the children to the seaside for the day, and to give them and the pensioners a party at Christmas.

Many collieries formed all kinds of sports teams, and several miners became professional footballers. Others went on to further education via the local technical colleges, and lack of opportunity was probably the only reason why university status was not achieved.

There was no doubt that miners' lives were hard, particularly in the early days, and though improving through the years, there was always the threat of injury, illness or even death hanging over their heads. They did a dirty, dangerous job, they worked hard and they played hard, and they were the backbone of the community.

This book serves to illustrate a lost way of life for a younger generation, to allow them to appreciate what it means when told that 'your granddad worked down the pit'.

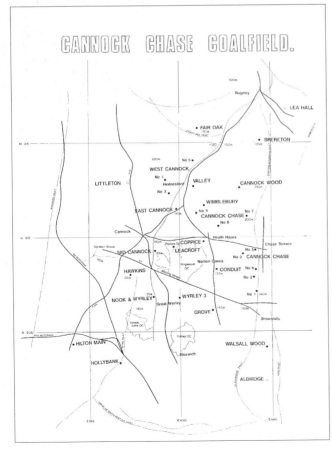

Map of the Cannock Chase coalfield

Above: Lea Hall Colliery opened 1960, closed 1990 – the last and most modern pit to be sunk.

Left: Map of the Cannock Chase coalfield indicating the position of pits in relation to the local area from the the late 1700s to the mid-1990s.

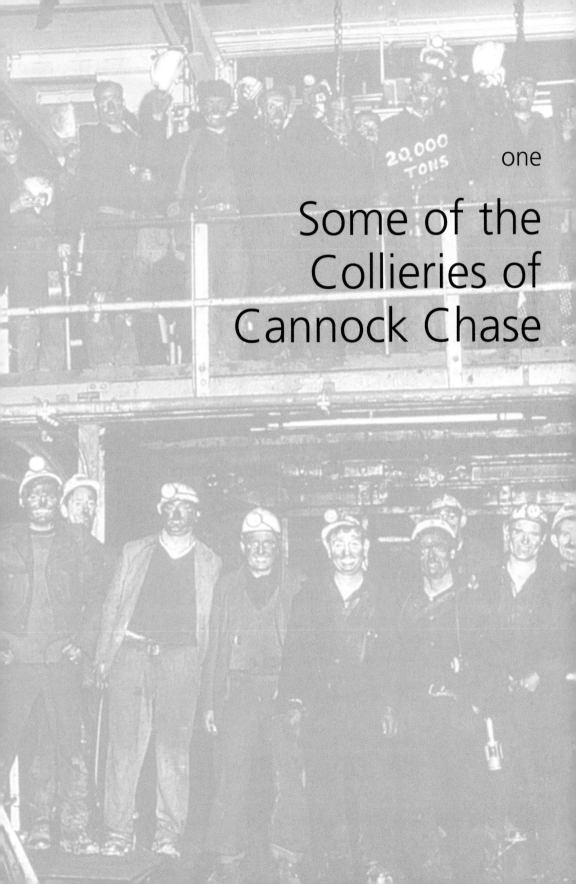

one

Some of the Collieries of Cannock Chase

A very early photograph of the Old Coppice Colliery, Cheslyn Hay (T.A. Hawkins).

Conduit Colliery, Walsall Road, Norton Canes. The miners were paid out of the window of the office on the roadside.

The Grove Pit, Brownhills; opened in 1869, closed in 1952.

The Pithead Aldridge Colliery.

The Coppice Colliery, Brereton, which opened in 1843. This was the scene of an accident on 15 February 1908. Three men drowned and many were injured when a huge torrent of water flooded part of the pit. This resulted in the closure of the pit with the loss of many jobs.

Brick Kiln Colliery, Brereton – opened 1820, closed 1960.

Wimblebury Colliery – opened 1872, closed 1962. Hednesford Hills are in the background.

West Cannock No. 5. Colliery, Brindley Heath, Hednesford. Opened 1914, closed 1982.

West Cannock Collieries Nos 1 and 2. They were built on land now known as Pye Green Valley, by West Cannock Colliery Co., which was founded in 1869. West Cannock 1 opened 1869, closing in 1958 and West Cannock 2 opened in 1869 and closed in 1887.

West Cannock No. 3. Colliery, Belt Road, Hednesford – opened 1869, closed 1949.

Cannock Wood Colliery, 1913. Opened 1864, closed 1973.

An early photograph of Coppice Colliery, Heath Hayes, also known as 'The Fair Lady'. Opened 1893, closed 1964.

No. 10 Colliery, Old Hednesford – opened 1850, closed 1908. The mineral railway line is in the middle distance, with Littleworth Road and Hednesford Hills in the background.

No. 9 Colliery, Hednesford taken at the occasion of its reopening in 1935. It originally opened 1850 and closed 1952.

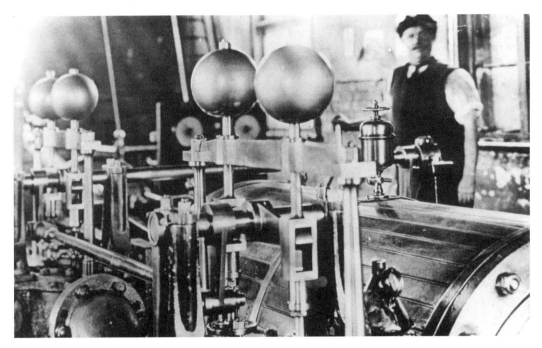

No. 8 Colliery opened 1868 – closed 1962. Pictured here is Mr Harley in the engine room of the Winding House. Note how clean and polished were all the moving parts.

East Cannock Colliery in the early 1900s. It opened in 1870 and closed in 1957.

Above: An aerial view of Mid Cannock Colliery, which opened in 1874 and closed in 1967. To the right of the photograph is the main Walsall to Cannock railway line.

Left: Littleton Colliery, Huntington – opened 1872, closed 1885, reopened 1897, closed 1993.

Above and below: The end of mining on Cannock Chase. The Bleak House Opencast, and one of the massive vehicles used in the operation. The land has now been returned to its former state.

Cannock Chase No. 2 – 'The Fly'. Note the double lamps in the right-hand corner of the photograph – it was the first pit in the country to be lit by electricity.

Mr Tooth – winding at Brereton Colliery, 1960.

Above: 'Topping out' the pithead at Hawkins No. 2 shaft in the early 1900s.

Left: Outside West Cannock No. 5's tub repair shop in 1940. From left to right, standing: Ray Pickett, Ted Grant. Kneeling: Jack Jones, Jim Hickinbottom.

West Cannock No.5. From left to right, back row: Jack Jones, Dick Seymour, Jack Brown, Bill Deakin. Front row: George Taylor, Joe Jackson, Arnold Miles.

West Cannock No. 5. From left to right: Roy Walklate, Gilbert Bolas, Arnold Miles, George Taylor, Dick Seymour, Gordon Bromley.

West Cannock No. 5, downcast pithead. From left to right: Jack Jones, Jack Houlston, Ern Lester, Arnold Miles.

West Cannock No. 5.
Barry Tatler (left) and Bill
Smith.

The Old Turbine House
and New Downcast
Winding House at West
Cannock No. 5. In the
foreground is electrician
Ron Wainwright.

A view of West Cannock
No. 5 showing new
powder magazine, stores,
workshops and garage.
In the distance can be
seen the hangars of RAF
Hednesford.

Left: The construction of the receiving frame for the downcast pit bottom at West Cannock No. 5. From left to right, back row: Joe Smith, Ern Lester, Mike Jones, Bernard Deakin, -?-, Harry Carter. Front row: Gilbert Bolas, Arnold Miles.

Below: West Cannock No. 5 – as viewed from the downcast headgear, which itself is casting a shadow at the bottom of the photograph. This scene shows the upcast headgear, conveyors to the coal preparation plant, sidings and the locomotive shed.

Above: The receiver for pit bottom being assembled on the surface at West Cannock No. 5.

Left: Preparing the Westinghouse framework for the pit bottom at West Cannock No. 5. From left to right: Jack Jones, Joe Evans, Gilbert Bolas, Arnold Miles.

A safety aid photograph from the 1970s showing an incorrect way of loading a drum of oil to go down Littleton pit.

A safety aid photograph showing a man repairing a machine in unsafe position. The bucket should have been propped. This was taken at the rear of Littleton pit workshop during the 1970s.

The stockyard at Cannock Wood Colliery – waiting to be scrapped.

In the showers at Valley Colliery, Hednesford. From left to right: Les Witton (Deputy), Bill Crabtree (Deputy), Cyril Ingle (Deputy), Jack Boden (Deputy), Wilf Borton (Electrician), Mot Seager (Deputy), Bill Newman (Deputy), Keith Davies (Deputy).

Above: Cannock Chase Colliery in the 1880s. The roof is being ripped to widen and raise the horse road.

Left: A shot hole is being drilled using an Eliott machine at Hawkin's Colliery in 1911. From left to right: Jack Snape, Fred Whitehouse, Ern Dawkins, Tom Smith (Colliery Deputy). Note the yardstick.

Opposite above: Quarterly surveyors from Birmingham surveying the boundaries in the 1880s.

Opposite below: 6's Robin's showing main roadway. Back ripping operations normally were carried out on the night shift to maintain roadway, giving sufficient height and clearance for coal on the conveyor to travel (Littleton colliery).

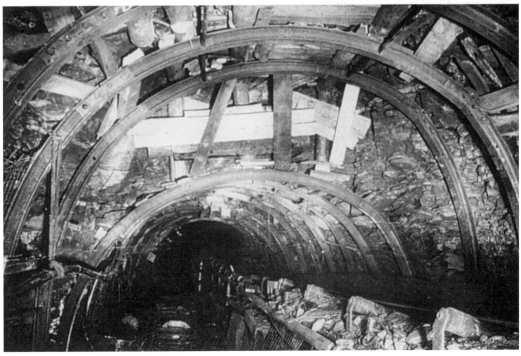

5's Robin's – No. 2 shaft at Littleton Colliery showing a miner digging coal at the tailgate to make it stable for the coal shearer machine and chain conveyor to be pushed over ready for the next cut. Note the powered supports used to support the roof.

Underground at Littleton Robin's – the main gate being driven. Note the wooden support on two steel girders and also the roof supported by 'horsehead' girders. The miner is trimming the rockface prior to drilling.

A new conveyor system at Littleton Colliery in the 1960s.

A view of the packing of rock used to support the roadway as the face advances at Littleton Colliery.

Horace Spruce cleaning a battery at Littleton No. 2 pit in January 1954.

A roadheading machine used to ventilate the pit.

The underground loco shed at Littleton No. 3's pit.

Salvage operations at Littleton Colliery 5's Robin's in the 1970s.

Above: Concrete blocks for shuttering around the shaft at Littleton Colliery.

Left: The start of sinking the Staple shaft at Littleton Colliery, 1970s.

Finishing the sinking at Littleton Colliery.

Lea Hall Colliery, the last pit on the Cannock Chase coalfield, was opened in 1960 and closed in 1990. What a comparison to the earlier pits!

Above: An underground firefighting point at Littleton No. 2's pit bottom.

Left: An official, wearing a self-rescuer, showing how to test for gas in the 1950s. Note the style of helmet, which dates back to the 1950s.

Above: A team at Littleton Colliery celebrate a 5.2 tonnes one-man shift.

Left: Lea Hall Colliery reaching is first target of 20,000 tons in one week in 1960.

In April 1981, four seven-man teams at West Cannock No. 5. Colliery established a new world tunnelling record of 251.4 metres in five days. The men worked round the clock with a 120hp British-built machine to achieve the new world record. It produced 1,200 tonnes of coal and involved the setting up of 253 steel supports weighing a total of 64 tonnes. Regrettably there is no photograph to record the occasion.

Above: Other members of the Littleton team below.

Left: Littleton Colliery record breakers: 100 metres in seven days. Included are: E. Walker, D. Allport, Deputy, J. Kalinski, J. Williscroft.

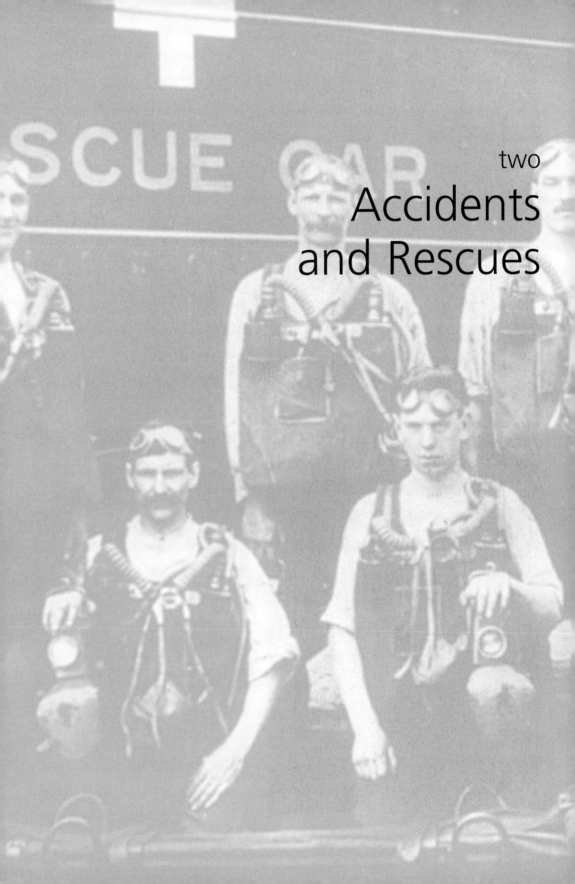

two

Accidents and Rescues

Old Hednesford Colliery Disaster (Cannock Chase No. 9), 14 December, 1911. Five miners were killed: Jacob Ward aged forty-nine – married with a big family; William Baugh aged twenty-seven – single; William Bradbury aged nineteen – supported his widowed mother; William Reeves aged forty-eight – married with one adult daughter; Tom Stokes aged forty-two – married.

At about noon a fire broke out. Huge volumes of smoke indicated to the sixty men working in the bass seam that they were in danger. All but five of the men made it to safety. Four of the deceased made the effort to follow but were beaten back by the fire, which was supposed to have started in the lamphouse situated 20 yards from the bottom of the shaft, the shaft being 250 yards deep. Tom Stokes, who had come safely to the pit bottom from No. 10 stall, pulled off his coat and said 'I will go' – he never came back.

One of the rescue party, made up of men who had just escaped, described it as like 'a burning furnace – impossible to get through'. Fifteen horses were also burnt alive. The fire raged unabated for many hours.

News of the accident spread quickly and a large crowd, including the anxious relatives of the victims, gathered around the pit head.

The inquest was held at the Anglesey Hotel as it was central and more convenient for the jury.

Old Hednesford Colliery Disaster

Above: Old Hednesford Colliery, with crowds of anxious miners, their wives and relatives waiting for news of the survivors, if any.

Left: George Archer, seen with his granddaughter Joan Bull, at his home in Mount Side Street, Hednesford, was present at the inquest in the capacity of fireman. Early in their marriage his wife had taught him to read so that he could pass his fireman's exams. He was down the pit with the Under Manager at the time of the fire but could do nothing to save the lives of the five men. He was greatly distressed by this situation, and newspapers were kept away from his young daughter to prevent her from reading about the disaster. To his great relief he was found innocent of any neglect. He was very much a family man, and outside work, took a great deal of care to look clean and tidy. He was noted for wanting every light on in the house during darkness because, as he said, 'you spend enough of your life in the dark'.

Left: John Haycock, on the doorstep of his home in Church Street, Chadsmoor. A young married man with the first of four children when this photograph was taken, he had his left leg amputated above the knee when it was crushed by a tub whilst working down the pit. It was replaced with a wooden stump strapped on at the waist, and it meant that for the rest of his life he walked with the aid of a walking stick. The accident made it impossible for him to carry on with his job as a miner but fortunately, despite high unemployment at the time, he secured a situation as an insurance agent, walking the streets of Chadsmoor to collect money from his customers, who knew him as 'Peggy Haycock'. It was a common sight to see men in the community with limbs missing.

Below: Hednesford Accident Home, situated in Littleworth Road, Hednesford. This was opened on 20 July 1896. The matron was Miss Wilkins in 1903, succeeded by Miss Beelestore in 1907 and Miss Annie Blakemore until 1950.

Above: One of the rooms inside Hednesford Accident Home – note the miners suffering from head injuries.

Left: W.F.G. Bagnall was Miners Agent from 1930 until he was forced to retire during the 1940s. On 16 May 1933 there was a mining disaster at West Cannock No.5's Colliery. He helped the widows to acquire compensation and they presented him with a gold pocket watch – the inscription reads:

W.C.C. No.5 Pit Disaster, May 16th 1933, Presented to W.F.G. Bagnall (Miners Agent) By the widows of Jos. Williams, S. Gwilt, B Cornwall, J. William and C. Turnock – In Appreciation of Service Rendered Oct. 11th 1933

The watch is still in the possession of the family.

FATAL ACCIDENTS AT CANNOCK CHASE COLLIERIES
(PRIOR TO NATIONALISATION IN 1947)

VALLEY COLLIERY

10.12.1882	Jim Francis aged 43 years – Run over by tubs, lost both legs
18.8.1883	Jim Gratton aged 25 years – Fall of rock in stall
15.9.1883	John Smith aged ? – Crushed between wall and wagons
26.2.1901	Joseph Lee aged 58 years – Fall of rock in stall
14.10.1902	Charles Fowler aged 17 years – Run over by full tubs
8.11.1902	Maurice Davies aged 37 years – Scalded by burst pipe in boiler house
17.2.1910	Joe Clements aged 17 years – Crushed by runaway tubs in Jig
9.3.1913	Arthur Hyden aged 18 years – Fall of rock in roadway
6.4.1913	George Mathews aged 31 years – Fall of rock in stall
22.4.1914	Andrew Peake aged 21 years – Fall of rock in stall
16.3.1923	Tom Ellwell aged 61 years – Crushed between tub and tree
7.10.1924	George Mabberly aged 45 years – Fall of rock in stall
15.7.1925	Francis Gretton aged 49 years – Crushed between tub and girder
26.09.1925	James Tatler aged ? – Fall of rock in stall
01.4.1936	Bill Jones aged 45 years – Fall of rock in rock heading
11.3.1939	Charles Alcott aged ? – Fall of rock whilst cutting coal
July 1942	Albert Ryan aged 48 years – Run away tubs in east deep hill
June 1946	Bernard Thacker aged 42 years – Died from head injuries in 1924

WIMBLEBURY COLLIERY

09.10.1902	Jim Morgan aged 67 years – Caught up in screen machinery
04.09.1909	Alfred Walsh aged 43 years – Crushed between buffers on wagons
09.11.1910	Fred Heath aged 15 years – Head crushed between full tubs
02.05.1912	Joe Timmins aged 61 years – Fall of rock in roadway
29.06.1912	George Hartshorne 15 years – Kicked in abdomen by horse
06.11.1919	Dan Allsopp aged 62 years – Fell off railway wagons
17.01.1924	George Seabury aged 18 years – Fall of rock in roadway
14.06.1927	John Wilkes aged 37 years – Cage crashed into pit bottom
14.06.1927	Bill Harrison aged 37 years – Cage crashed into pit bottom
07.02.1936	Bill Colley aged 54 years – Slipped down incline

WEST CANNOCK NO. 1

08.03.1895	Henry Morden aged 20 years – Fall of rock
08.03.1895	Bill Maund aged 20 years – Fall of rock
11.01.1896	Isaac Darrell aged 37 years – Burnt in gas explosion
24.05.1897	Harry Dyke aged 33 years – Pinned against pipe by roof fall
10.12.1898	George Nicholls aged 24 years – Fall of rock in stall
12.05.1900	George Richards aged 16 years – Fall of rock in stall
14.01.1903	J. Orme aged 22 years – Fall of rock – died 8.1.1904
24.09.1903	W. Rogers aged 36 years – Fall of rock in stall
17.02.1907	Joe Farmer aged 58 years – Injured sidening tubs
30.06.1910	Alfred Beeston aged 39 years – Crushed against girder
02.07.1910	Jim Bradbury aged 25 years – Fall of rock in stall

Col-Sgt Bird, F. Company of the Volunteers, was buried in Cannock Cemetery with full military honours and in the presence – and amid universal respect – of between 5-6,000 spectators.

The Volunteers marched with reversed arms and unsheathed swords while the band played *The Dead March* against the measured beat of muffled drums, making a great impression on the thousands who crowded the streets.

A full report in the *Hednesford Advertiser* dated 9.3.1895 sold out and was reprinted the following Monday.

Col-Sgt Bird's widow and ten children were left without a breadwinner, so one of the sons went to seek some kind of help from the colliery in the form of an allowance of coal. The answer was: 'A dead mon doe need coal'. This son later became a member of the Communist party!

07.10.1911	Bill Westwood aged 43 years – Fall of rock in stall
23.01.1912	Tom Lane aged 69 years – Crushed by railway wagons in thick fog
21.02.1912	Jim Bromley aged 16 years – Run over by horse drawn tubs
21.04.1914	Ted Hayward aged 46 years – Fall of rock in stall
20.01.1915	Joshua Thomas aged 50 years – Electric shock
08.02.1915	Bill Drury aged 32 years – Riding empty tubs – fell and hit full tubs
28.04.1918	Fred Payne aged 31 years – Fall of rock in roadway
25.08.1918	Bill Sambrooks aged 41 years – Run over by full tubs
04.01.1921	Herbert Watson aged 46 years – Crushed whilst oiling machinery
28.01.1921	Bill Watts aged 45 years – Fall of rock in roadway
04.01.1924	Jim Denny aged 61 years – Fumes from gob fire
19.01.1927	John Powell aged 60 years – Fall of rock in stall
16.11.1936	Jeremiah Wood aged 33 years – Buried by 7 tons of bind
13.03.1937	Joe Moseley aged 58 years – Fall of rock in stall
06.04.1940	Frank Taylor aged 53 years – Run over by runaway empty tubs
04.09.1945	John Caswell aged 60 years – Fall of rock on face
04.09.1945	Tom Shaw aged 32 years – Fall of rock on face

WEST CANNOCK NO. 2

05.11.1879	Bill Brindley aged ? – Fall of rock in stall
01.06.1882	Alex Downes aged 14 years – Crushed between buffers (worked 2 weeks)
22.12.1931	Ted Bird aged ? – Fall of rock in stall
27.09.1938	Len Dawson aged 17 years – Fall of rock broke his neck
12.12.1940	Henry Wood aged 66 years – Fall of side coal on face
01.10.1942	Bill Bradford aged 43 years – Fell 100 yards down shaft freeing cage

WEST CANNOCK NO. 3

26.02.1895	Colour Sergeant Bird aged 58 years – Working in pit shaft (leaves 10 children)

15.06.1901	Bill Taylor aged 54 years – Fall of rock in roadway
23.05.1913	Solomon Price aged 25 years – Fall of rock in stall
29.04.1919	Jim Everan aged 30 years – Fall of rock in roadway
05.02.1921	Francis Weetman aged 51 years – Crushed between cage and girder
14.10.1924	W. Lear aged ? – Crushed between wall & railway wagons
05.12.1928	Ernest Benton aged 31 years – Mangled in coal cutting machine
06.09.1930	Richard Williams aged 48 years – Fall of rock in stall
13.05.1935	John Hubbard aged 45 years – Fall of rock on coal face left 8 children
13.05.1935	Richard Hubbard aged 40 years – Fall of rock on coal face
13.05.1935	John Briggs aged 25 years – Fall of rock on coal face
23.12.1942	Walter Thorne aged 41 years – Fall of rock in roadway
22.08.1947	George Thacker aged 45 years – Fall of rock in roadway

WEST CANNOCK NO. 4

29.03.1881	Tom Davies aged / Gas explosion in coal heading
06.12.1890	John Garbett aged 29 years Fall of rock in roadway
03.12.1895	Alfred Wilde aged 14 years Fell off railway wagon
07.11.1899	John Morris aged 32 years – Fall of coal in stall
08.02.1900	Walter Johnson aged 40 years – Buried by roof fall at junction
02.02.1914	David Bowater aged 37 years – Run over by railway wagons
02.12.1917	Alfred Fowler aged 42 years – Run over by full tubs in incline
1927	Mr Bennett aged ? – Threw himself down shaft

WEST CANNOCK NO. 5

1901	John Deakin aged 36 years – Hit by piece of wood/circular saw
01.07.1914	Noah Davies aged 41 years – Fall of coal on coal face
21.03.1916	Fred Jones aged ? – Trapped between cage and shaft
02.07.1921	Charles Stokes aged 52 years – Fall of rock in roadway
24.12.1922	John Gittings aged 18 years – Fall of rock in roadway
05.12.1930	John Cadman aged 35 years – Fall of rock in stall
23.11.1940	George Robson aged ? – Run over by tub in jig
29.09.1922	Sid Turner aged 17 years – Run over by runaway tubs
06.02.1924	Tom Shale aged 44 years –. Fall of rock in stall
29.09.1925	Bill Harvey aged 38 years – Fall of rock in stall
29.09.1925	Albert Morgan aged 46 years – Fall of rock in stall
28.03.1926	Henry Stibbs aged 39 years – Head injuries received 15 years previous
31.01.1929	George Loverock aged 40 years – Fall of rock
28.10.1929	Henry Caswell aged 37 years – Mutilated by compressed air cutter
17.07.1930	Ted Stevens aged 28 years – Found in gas filled waste
06.10.1932	Tom Summerfield aged 30 years – Fall of rock
04.06.1936	Fred Brearly aged 64 years – Fall of rock
31.12.1936	Charles Brindley aged 47 years – Fall of rock
31.12.1938	John Sheratt aged 43 years – Fall of rock
31.12.1938	John Cooper aged 54 years – Fall of rock
20.08.1939	John Pearce aged 44 years – Fall of rock in waste
16.09.1944	Ben Bishop aged 44 years – Hit by rock – shot firing
16.05.1933	Sam Gwilt aged ? – Firedamp explosion, shallow seam, upcast pit
16.05.1933	Charles Turnock aged ? – 8.30 a.m. 15 other miners were injured

16.05.1933	Ben Cornwall aged ? – Either gassed or burnt
16.05.1933	Joe Williams aged ?
16.05.1933	John Williams aged ?
16.05.1933	Bill Higgs aged ?
16.05.1933	Two pit ponies

EAST CANNOCK COLLIERY

06.07.1880	Tom Rowley aged 21 years – Fall of rock in stall
13.05.1881	Sam Rowley aged ? – Run over by tubs
21.11.1891	Fred Hempson aged 19 years – Run over by horse drawn tubs
07.04.1892	Jom Burns aged 59 years – Gassed in gob fire
07.04.1892	Jim Davies aged 21 years – Gassed in gob fire
06.01.1894	John Pay aged 17 years – Run over by full tubs in jig
03.10.1894	Solomon Woodall aged 34 years – Gas explosion caused by candle
30.06.1895	Bill Horton aged 18 years – Run over by horse drawn tubs
09.10.1896	Arthur Watkins aged 14 years – Run over by 5 tubs on rope haulage
10.12.1897	Alfred Riley aged ? – Explosion caused by naked light
16.01.1898	Albert Robinson aged 14 years – Crushed by tubs against air doors
10.10.1903	Walter Richardson aged 22 years – Crushed by tubs broke his neck
17.12.1903	John Jones aged 43 years – Fall of rock in stall
21.12.1903	Sylvanos Benton aged 23 years – Crushed by tubs in jig
14.06.1908	Joe Kinsey aged 34 years – Fall of rock in stall
27.07.1908	Joe Churchill aged 53 years – Fall of rock in stall
03.12.1912	John Jones aged 20 years – Trapped between tubs and cage
16.09.1920	Tom Williscroft aged 23 years – Crushed by roadside and tubs
27.02.1921	Jacob Clift aged 60 years – Fall of rock in stall
09.11.1922	Bill Slack aged 39 years – Fall of rock in stall
21.08.1928	Jim Gibbons aged 69 years – Hit head against tubs
22.02.1929	Jim Molineoux aged 20 years – Lifting full tubs – died 14 April
03.04.1931	Bill Fleming aged 51 years – Hit by runaway tub on dirt mound
23.11.1940	John Dudson aged ? – Run over by tub of ashes
24.06.1947	Bob Kenny aged 30 years – Fall of rock on coal face

CANNOCK WOOD COLLIERY

14.02.1883	F. Matthias aged 67 years – Fall of rock in stall
19.12.1884	John Cole aged 32 years – Hit by lump of coal in stall
01.06.1900	Bill Harvey aged 55 years – Hit by rock, shot firing
07.09.1900	John Whitehouse aged 15 years – Fall of rock in roadway
25.09.1900	Isaiah Whitehouse aged 36 years – Fall of rock in stall
23.03.1901	Sam Robinson aged 25 years – Run over by loco 'Messenger'
01.12.1909	John Brown aged 27 years – Fall of rock in stall
21.06.1911	Mark Cox aged 33 years – Fall of rock in stall
23.05.1913	Ted Walker aged 41 years – Fall of rock in stall
20.02.1914	George Watton aged 33 years – Trapped between tub and sprag
14.08.1915	Tom Tipton aged 55 years – Fall of rock in stall
13.11.1917	Jim Ashley aged 15 years – Head crushed between tub & tree
10.05.1918	Harry Harvey aged 42 years – Fall of coal in stall
10.12.1919	Walter Hyden aged 37 years – Fall of coal in stall

30.04.1920	Enoch Oldacre aged 69 years – Run over by runaway tubs in jig
20.12.1922	Bill Jarvis aged 23 years – Buried in fall of coal in stall
13.02.1924	Bert Elsmore aged 30 years – Fall of rock in stall
14.04.1924	Frank Chapman aged 27 years – Fall of rock in stall
05.10.1926	Richard Winfindale aged 33 years – Fall of coal in stall
08.10.1926	Charles Taylor aged ? – Fall of coal in stall
03.05.1927	Jacob Biggs aged 61 years – Fall of rock in stall
07.12.1928	Ben Bailey aged 68 years – Run over by locomotive
27.08.1929	Henry Rowley aged 52 years – Fall of coal in stall
11.10.1929	James Wall aged 58 years – Fall of coal in stall
02.09.1931	Bill Bailey aged 55 years – Fall of coal in stall
02.09.1931	Jessie Bailey (son) 20 years – Fall of coal in stall
27.10.1933	Henry Marsh aged 62 years – Crushed finger – died pneumonia
06.10.1934	Richard Tilsley aged 64 years – Fall of rock
29.10.1936	Ernest Bradbury aged 69 years – Fell off locomotive
21.06.1939	George Rowley aged 53 years – Fall of rock
20.10.1939	Arthur Binfield aged 32 years – Fall of rock

Cannock Chase Rescue
Brigade No. 6 – no names.

This may be a team from
West Cannock 5's – note
the webbing headgear.

Passing out in 1926. From left to right, back row: -?-, Jos. Payton, -?-, -?-, Mr Street. Front row: Alf Newell, -?-, Cyril Hopkins. Again note the webbing headgear.

Cannock & Rugeley Old Coppice Colliery Rescue Brigade.

Coppice (The Fair Lady) Heath Hayes No. 5. Rescue Brigade.

From left to right, back row: Frank Hales, Jos. Payton, Jesse Brough, Mr Street, Alec Jeavons. Front row: Len Angel, -?-, Bill Thorn.

Cannock & Leacroft Rescue Team – Winners of Cannock Chase Coalowners Rescue Cup in 1936.

Passing out, 1937. There were only six men in a rescue team, although there are seven in this pose. At the bottom right is a first aid box from the Crimean War made of cow hide, while in the centre is the reviving kit. From left to right, back row: Harry Wilkes, Jos. Payton, -?-, Jack Allsopp, Mr Street, -?-. Front row: -?-, Reg Fletcher, Frank Wilkes.

Coppice Colliery Rescue Team, 1938. From left to right, back row: Vic. Carrier, Jos. Payton, Henry Lee, -?-, Mr Street -?-. Front row: -?-, T. Mills.

Presentation at Hednesford Rescue Station, Victoria Street, Hednesford. Third from right, back row: Richard Payne. From left to right, front row: Jonathon Hunter jnr, Herbert Bird (with cup), Harry Saffhill, Jonathon Hunter snr, -?-, -?-.

West Cannock Colliery 5's. On the far right is Mr Colburn.

1985 Area Winners, Lea Hall D team. From left to right, back row: Steve Perrin, Ray Cooper, Bob Carroll. Front row: Barry Pickering, Robert Edge, Jon Houston.

MINER'S PRAYER

Arv cum terday ter say thank yer God,
Fer all yove dun fer me,
Fer me early mornin brekfust un me daily cupper tea,
Yow care fer me when arm down that ole in a werld so black,
Un wen ar count me blessin there ay much that i lack,
Ar no ar cuss un swear a bit, call out yer name in vain,
But ar know at times yow shut yer ears cus yow no arm very plain,
Yow gid we trees that med the coal,
That with pick un swet we cut,
Un then the water which med the road to tek it up the cut,
We see the wunder of yer hand in tunnels black and deep,
There ay no sunshine or fallin rain,
But still yer harvest reap,
We seek yer cumfert in sorry times,
When roof begins to fall,
We call yer name in terror,
To watch over one un all,
Un when we see light er day,
As up the shaft we cum,
We say thankyer god we're up again,
Another day is dun.

AER REG.   B.E.M.

The submarine HMS *Thetis*, completed in March 1939, sank on 1 June 1939 with the loss of ninety-nine lives. Divers recovered sixty-four bodies but thirty-five bodies were still in a sealed chamber within the submarine. A report prepared by Superintendent J. Payton from Hednesford Rescue Station tells of how rescue men from Cannock Chase coalfield were called in to recover these remaining bodies.

Instructions were received on 28 October 1939 to send the following six men to Holyhead, one man from each colliery: T. Forsyth (Captain) – Brereton Colliery, S.J. Wall – Conduit Colliery, J. Hyden – Cannock & Rugeley Colliery, H. Saffhill – Cannock & Leacroft Colliery, J. B. Calo – West Cannock Colliery, C. Holgate (Lieutenant) – Mid Cannock. One man was selected from each colliery so that no pit was without a rescue team.

On 10 November 1939, the *Thetis* was put into dry dock at Holyhead and the team was told to be ready to enter the vessel by 1.30 p.m. The weight of the bodies made very heavy work but seven bodies were recovered by Cannock Chase men, then the navy, trained by the miners, brought out nine more bodies. The next morning the remaining nineteen bodies were recovered.

Cannock & Leacroft Ambulance teams, 1911. Unfortunately there are no names for the men in the photograph.

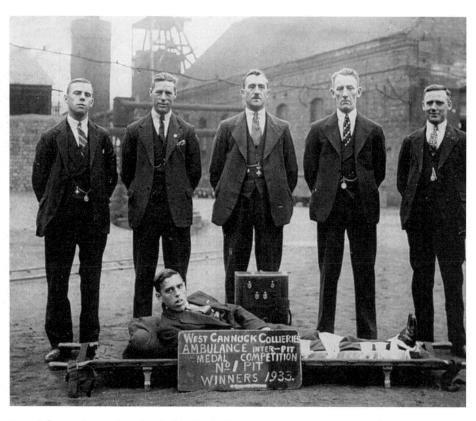

From left to right, standing: Jim Smith, -?-, Colliery Manager, -?-, George Woodhead. Lying down: the patient?

Mid Cannock Ambulance team 1919 – no names.

This photograph was taken in Walkmill Lane, Bridgtown, outside the premises of Cannock Agricultural.
The known members of the St John's Ambulance are, from left to right: May Bates, Frank ?

An Ambulance Supper in the 1940s for T.A. Hawkins' Cannock Old Coppice. From left to right, back row: Mrs Adams, –?–, –?–, Rex Adams, Mrs Wilson, Ray Wilson, Arthur Wilkes, Fred Wilkes, Harry Cadman. Middle row: –?–, Mrs Morgan, Stan Morgan, Mrs Thacker, Bill Thacker. Front row: George Bradshaw, Mrs Bradshaw, Mrs Dutton, Horace Dutton, –?–.

West Cannock No. 3. Ambulance and First Aid Class, 1928. From left to right, middle row: Arthur Tatler, –?–, Joe Bailey, –?–, Albert Hargreaves. Sixth from left, back row: Ted Bevan.

Littleton First Aid Team behind the Baths at Littleton Colliery in the 1960s. From left to right: –?–, Alan Slade, Alec Jeavons (Safety Officer) Bob Stephenson, Johnny Mears, 'Macka' Matthews (patient).

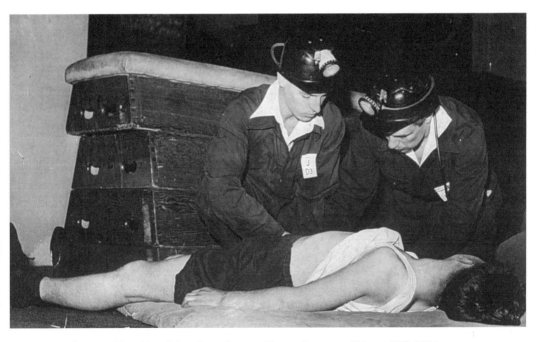

First aid competition. Examining the patient are Horace Spruce and Trevor Hill, 1957.

Littleton Junior First Aid Team, 1954/55. From left to right: Jack Cumberbatch (Manager), Alan Slade (Captain) Alec Jeavons (Trainer) Trevor Hill, Jim Linskill, Maurice Stokes, Horace Spruce, Len Angell (Trainer). In 1937 Littleton Colliery's First Aid Team won the district top award the 'Cannock Chase Shield' captained by Mr Joe Woodhall, a miner for more than forty years. He won his first competition medal in 1927, only a year after he started first aid.

This photograph, taken in the canteen at Littleton Colliery, shows the first safety competition prizes for the Staffordshire Area. From left to right, back row: –?–, –?–, –?–, Alf Powick (Under Manager). Front row: Arthur Smith, –?–, Colin Plant, –?–, Mr Barber (Manager), Jack Hayward.

A party of Safety Officers from other industries on a visit to Littleton Colliery in the 1970s. Taken outside No. 2. pit top before going underground. On the extreme right is Ron Brookes.

A photograph taken at the back of the social centre at Littleton Colliery, with Limepit Lane in the background. Area Manager Mr Wright (known as Nippy) and Mr Barber, Manager, holding the winners' certificate of the National Safety Competition, with Ron Brookes (Safety Officer) holding a cheque for £6,500. This money was used for purchasing prizes for safety awards the following year. D. Williamson, Peter Timpson and Sid Bailey (all present in the photograph) had full attendance in that year. Others in the photograph are Arthur Felton, Norman Pearce, John Taylor, Bill Bentley, Arthur Smith, Jack Hughes and Joe Marriott.

Safety Quiz team to area finals at Stoke-on-Trent taken in 1971/2 at Littleton Colliery canteen, Littleton versus West Cannock 5's. Back row, from left to right: Johnny Gough,(West Cannock 5's) –?– (–?–, –?–, –?–, –?–, –?– North Staffs team) Ron Brookes (–?–, North Staffs) A. Felton, Carl Felton. Front row, from left to right: Tommy Weston, Arthur Wilkes, Billy Dawes, Johnny Ball, Joe Marriott – all Littleton team.

Miners convalesce at Margate in 1920. Second from left, back row: Reuben Jones.

Weston-super-Mare Convalescent Home, 1941. Included are, from left to right, back row: Harry Edwards, -?-, Mr Hickinbottom.

A party of miners, mainly from Cannock Chase Collieries, at Weston-super-Mare Convalescent Home, *c.* 1958. Centre, back row: Ron Brookes. Far left, third row: J. Evans.

Left: Weston–super–Mare Convalescent Home.
George Woodhead (left) and Charlie Dawes.

Below: Convalescent Home, North Shore,
Blackpool.

three

Sport

The location of this ceremony may be Heath Hayes Park. The lady behind the table is the widow of R.W. Hanbury, who sank the Coppice Colliery at Heath Hayes in 1894. She cut the first turf and always took an interest, driving to the mine in her carriage, looking very regal in her distinctive hat. During the 1912 strike a boiler was put in the wagon shop and she dished out soup to the men. She was also responsible for organising trips to Blackpool for the miners and their families and bonuses for good production. The colliery was always called 'The Fair Lady' by those who worked there.

Was this the same event? The clothes are the same, indicating that it was probably the early 1900s. The photograph appears to show a winning bowls team.

Cannock Chase Colliery FC during the 1935/36 season. This team was famous for appearing on a cigarette card. From left to right, back row: C. Bailey, P. Cheetham, W. Williamson. J. Dennis (Chairman) G. Lewis, W. Earp, R. James, T. Williamson (Secretary) G. Reynold, H. Wright (Trainer). Middle Row L-R A. Proffitt, A. Whittaker, P. Coyne, F. Eccleshall, W. Lewis, H. Wilton. Front row: H. Heath, W. Hassall, B. Maiden, W. Tasker, W. Evans. They won the Walsall & District League, the Walsall Senior Cup and the Walsall Charity Cup.

In the 1949/50 season this team won the Lonsdale Cup, Cannock Charity Cup, and were Division 1 and 2 winners. Included in the picture are Harry Parsons (Manager) Frank Whitehouse, Bill Dyas, Jack Dyas, Logan Crowder, George Todd, Chris Duffy, Paddy Hegatty, McCormack. Note the pit stack and mound in the background.

The football team of the Victoria Working Men's Club, Belt Road, Hednesford. From left to right, back row: Alf Lane, Ben New, Arthur Deakin, Doug Westwood, Eric Baker, Bernard Payne, Jack Maddox, Bernard Ford, Sam Spooner, Wilf Hotchkiss, Ralph Matthews, Harold Steventon, Walter Westwood. Front row: Mr Hassall, Charlie Deakin, ? Woodhall, Bert Thompson, Eric Spooner, Harry Dyke, Len Martin. The coal trucks and pit mound in the background is now an open landscaped green space called Pye Green Valley.

St Chad's football team, 1948/49. From left to right, back row: -?-, -?-, Ray 'Nobby' Cooper, Arnie Wilkes, Ernie Taylor, Eric 'Bola' Saunders, Roy ? , John 'Paddy' Bagley, Jackie Jones, Cliff 'Masha' Marsh, Nock Bailey, -?-.

Rawnsley Village Youth Club football teams, winners of the Cannock & District Youth League in 1950/51. This photograph was taken outside Stacey's Photographic Studio, McGhie Street, Hednesford. From left to right, back row: Harry Edwards, (Secretary) Len Burton, ? Parker, ? Davies, Gordon Watkins, Bill Gallear, Ray West, Graham Brookes. Front row, from left to right: Jim Brookes, Powell, Eric Mear, Bob Brooks, Gordon Tildesley, John Brooks.

Wimblebury FC, winners of the Cannock Youth League, 1953/54. From left to right, back row: G. Parker, R. Robinson, B. Vernon, E. Suffolk, S. Robinson, R. Hall. Front row: G. Hindley (Referee) S. Davis, G. Branswick. R. Strudwick, L Whittaker, T. Whittaker, M. Harper (Trainer). Hednesford Hills and Littleworth Road are in the background.

North West Shallow, winners of West Cannock 5's Inter-District Knockout Competition in 1958. This photograph was taken outside West Cannock Sports and Social Club. From left to right: back row: Alan Watkins (Referee), -?-, -?-, -?-, Albert Dando, Bruce Molineaux, Sam Spooner. Front row: John Gough, Derek Lane, Bill Gough, -?-, -?-.

West Cannock 5's Colliery Inter-District Knockout Football Competition, 1957. The winners were North West Shallow and runners-up were Top Shallow. From left to right, back row: John Gough, Sam Spooner, Les Walsh, -?-, -?-, ? Whitehouse, -?-, Eric Whitehouse, Tom Jones, ? Whitehouse, -?-, -?-, -?-, Harry Edwards. Front row: -?-, -?-, John Clare, Bill Gough -?-, Albert Dando, Derek Lane, -?-, -?-. Spectators far back: Tom Ward, Dick Price. This photograph was also taken outside West Cannock Sports and Social Club.

This Sunday morning football team played Hednesford Territorial Army on Hednesford Park in 1942. This photograph was taken in Victoria Street, Hednesford, opposite the Drill Hall – note the rear of the houses in Station Road. From left to right, back row: -?-, Graham Brooks, Harold Crutchley, Ben Fowler, Front row: Arnie Miles, Dennis Lane, Harry Edward, Tom Jones, -?-, Gordon Watkins, Bert Jones.

The awards presentation at the 1958 Inter–District Knockout Football Competition at West Cannock Sports and Social Club. Pictured are Ern Wilkes, Bob Clemson, Mr Bullock, Mr Nicholas, Harry Edwards, Jack Miles, Mrs Rowley.

Another photograph of the 1958 prizes. From left to right, front row: Mr Bullock, Tom Ward, Colin Phillips, Dennis Phillips, Ron Shaw, Tony Smith, Jack Miles, 'Digger' Bailey. Middle row: Mr Nicholas, ? Palmer, ? Davies, -?-, Bob Clemson, Harold ?. Back row: Joe Roadway, Bill Hemmings, ? Bailey, Billy Chapman, Ken Birch. In background: Harry Edwards, Ben Fowler, -?-.

The winners and losers of the West Cannock No. 5 Colliery six-a-side cricket knockout competition at Hednesford Park, *c.* 1955. Winners were the loco engine drivers on the surface. From left to right, back row: Ken Onions, -?-, Ken Birch, -?-, -?-. Middle row: John Gough (Umpire), Harry Edwards, Ken Baker, Horace Thacker, Mr Nicholas, Sammy Smith, Bruce Molineaux, P. Smith, Jack Miles, Mr Hood (behind). Front row: Jack Phillips, Bill Hood.

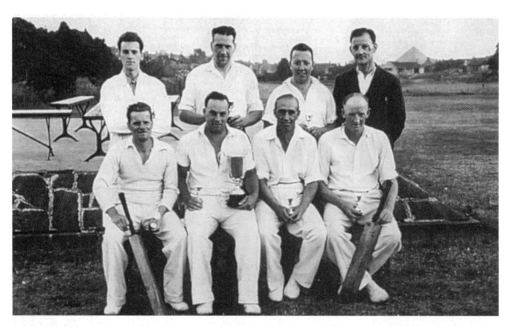

The winning team of that tournament. From left to right, back row: John Gough, Ken Birch, -?-, Harry Edwards. Front row: Ken Onions, Jack Phillips, Ken Baker, Horace Thacker. Note: behind the team can be seen the bandstand and in the distance is the East Cannock pit mound.

West Cannock Colliery Saturday cricket team in Hednesford Park, *c.* 1955. From left to right, back row: Harry Edwards, -?-, -?-, Tom Jones, Billy Chapman, Dennis Allsopp, Jack Phillips. Front row: Bill Hood, Denis Cope, Graham Brooks, Eric Gough, Dennis Tennant, Ruth Boonsley (scorekeeper).

The Cannock & Rugeley cricket team, 1950s. Among those in the photograph are Alf Prince, ? Lockley, Bill Rogers, Mr 'Cabby' Evans (Umpire), Ray West, ? Phillips and Ron Houlston.

West Cannock Sports and Social Club, West Cannock 5's six-a-side cricket knockout competition, 1959. The winners were Top Shallow, with West Shallow the runners-up. From left to right: Bill Hood, Ian Cooper, D. Langley, Ben Fowler, Bill Dando, Lance Shemwell, Harry Edwards, Dick Price Jr, Bill Chapman, Dereck Richards, George Clare, -?-, Alan Poole, -?-, Horace Rowley.

Cannock Wood Colliery tug-of-war team in the 1960s. The trainer was Geoff Evans. From front: H. Weaver, H. Salt, W. Cauchens, P. Liv, B. Salt. The anchorman was W. Forrester.

Hednesford Salvation Army Torchbearers table tennis team who were Cannock Youth Club's champions in 1954. From left to right, standing: Leon Mack, Reg Wood. Sitting: Maurice Baskeyfield, John Nicholls, John Baskeyfield, Geoff Benn.

WALSALL SENIOR CUP FINALS (involving Chase Collieries)

1926/27	Walsall FC 1 – 0 West Cannock Colliery
1929/30	West Cannock Colliery 2 – 1 Bloxwich Strollers
1930/31	Cannock Chase Colliery 3 – 2 Bloxwich Strollers
1931/32	Cannock Chase Colliery 4 – 2 Short Heath United
1934/35	Cannock Chase Colliery 2 – 2 Walsall Wood
1935/36	Cannock Chase Colliery 2 – 1 Wrockwardine Wood
1936/37	Cannock Chase Colliery 3 – 1 Wrockwardine Wood
1937/38	Cannock Chase Colliery 5 – 0 English Electric
1938/39	Cannock Chase Colliery 2 – 2 Sutton Town
1939/40	Cannock Chase Colliery 9 – 0 Rugeley St. Augustines

In the 1880s to 1890s teams like Walsall, Aston Villa, West Bromwich Albion, Wolverhampton Wanderers competed for this trophy.

WORKING THE PIT

I was looked upon as a lowly man
Part of bygone poverty plan,
But with sweat and patience my standard I raised
To be admired by many and my achievements praised,
But what was my future now gone from sight
The head gear wheels turning black diamonds so bright,
My years of work were just Gods lease
Today we have targets so shares may increase,
There would have been no coal board, budge or golden hole
If I had not scrawled and worked like a mole,
Yes my pits are all closed my ponies all gone
Yet still in my memory they linger on,
Each one a part of my work family tree
The ponies, the coal, forever with me.

Aer Reg (B.E.M.)

The last pony to be brought
out of Cannock Wood Colliery,
c. 1968. Safety Officer Eddie
Martin is holding the reins.

four

Transport

'Bob' at Cannock Wood Colliery. The name of the miner is unknown.

On 12 July 1924 at the Royal Show at Leicester West Cannock Collieries won first, second and third prizes for their ponies 'Norman', 'Smiler' and 'Haig'. The West Cannock Collieries owned 202 ponies and Headman was Mr Barfield.

At the Royal Show at Norwich in 1957 the Cannock Chase collieries were represented by 'Major' (East Cannock, keeper T. Marsh), 'Throstle' (Mid Cannock, keeper H. Tonks), 'Duke' (Cannock Wood, keeper R. Reade) and 'Laddie' (Valley, keeper K. Tinsley).

Among the participants at the Royal Show at Bristol in 1958 were 'Boxer' (Cannock Wood, keeper R. Reade), 'Mettle' (Valley, keeper K. Tinsley), 'Sandy' and 'Rex' (Mid Cannock, keeper H. Tonks).

Colonel Williamson's (managing director of Cannock & Rugeley Colliery Co. and colonel of the 5th Battalion South Staffs Territorial Regiment) pride and joy was 'Rawnsley Lad'.

Ponies were taken out of Cannock Chase Pits in April 1969.

Opposite above: 'Snap time' (or in other words – lunch time) at Hawkins Colliery in 1911. From left to right: Tom Smith (Colliery Deputy), his son in front, George Horney, Frank Siven, Cyril Dickinson, Frank Hunt, Matt Heinnigan. The two grey horses were used for pulling the tubs. Note the water bottle also used to hold cold tea, the hobnailed boots and the tub of coal. It is interesting to note that the horse seems to be the only one aware of the photographer. You can only imagine the mutterings among the men – 'tek no notice of 'im, with 'is newfangled contraption, 'e wants to get some real werk to 'is back'.

Opposite below: Mr Will Rowley, farrier at Coppice Colliery, photographed in 1913. He was also the village crier.

An early model of an engine with the name *Cannock Wood*. The names of the men are unknown.

A colliery locomotive crossing the road at the Cross Keys, Old Hednesford. It was taking the coal to the canal basin at East Cannock. On the left is the crossing keeper's house, which in the 1940s was manned by Mr and Mrs Lord. Imagine the congestion this would cause today on the road, which is now so busy.

The 'Paddy Train' running from Hednesford to Cannock Wood Colliery along the Rawnsley Road, *c.* 1938. The driver is T. Bradley. It is a Harrison 2-4-0 tank engine named *Hope*, which was built in 1875 by the Yorkshire Engine Company, Sheffield. This train was used to transport workmen from Hednesford to Cannock Wood Colliery.

The *Cannock Wood*, originally named *Burgundy*. This 0-6-0 saddle tank was purchased in 1926 by Cannock & Rugeley Colliery for £850 and sold to East Somerset in 1964.

Left: Kenneth Birch – a colliery engine driver – outside the Washery at West Cannock 5's in the early 1970s.

Below: The engine *Peckett* in the 1960s on West Cannock 5's railway. Posing in front are Kenneth Birch (centre) and Sid Hackett, Foreman (right). Terraced houses in Brindley Heath Road can just be seen on the left of the photograph with a lorry waiting for the weighbridge and landsale. On the right is one of the post-war houses in the same road.

No. 8. engine, possibly borrowed from Cannock & Rugeley Colliery. The tank is being filled with water via the hose by Mr Alf Lockett. The building in the background is 5's Washery.

Mr Kenneth Birch driving *Stafford*. This photograph is taken on 1's, 2's and 4's railways, with the pit mound just visible top right. It could be either Belt Road or Greenheath Road in background. Mr Birch learned to drive an engine with Mr Southall, the previous driver.

Above: No. 8. engine driven by Mr Kenneth Birch. The pieces of wood were collected when wagons were emptied to be used by the night shift, whose job it was to clean the engine and wheels and light the fire ready for work the next morning.

Left: This photograph was taken from Rugeley Road, with the main LMS line from Rugeley in the foreground. The engine is on West Cannock 5's line and in the background on the right is the landsale. The doors on the wagons are dropped open to empty coal into bags ready for sale. Note the floodlights.

The *Marquis*, a saddle tank locomotive which operated between 1840 and 1960.

Birch, a Littleton Colliery engine.

Mr Kenneth Birch (left) with *Peckett* being filled with water and Mr Alf Lockett with No. 8.

Holly Bank, another Littleton engine.

Locomotive No. 4, *Rawnsley* at Wimblebury sidings in 1947. The men are W. Martin (driver), F. Boden (shunter), W. Witton (Despatch Clerk). The *Rawnsley* was a saddle tank engine built in 1875 and belonged to Cannock & Rugeley Colliery.

five

Religion

The period from 1880 to 1893 was a time of great religious activity within the area surrounding the collieries of Cannock Chase. The Church of England, various denominational chapels and the Salvation Army were all active and supported by a large number of miners and their families.

Albert Foster [a local miner] born in 1866 in Heath Hayes, states that while working down the pit horse driving, some of the men were so interested about us lads they used to get us together at 'snap time' and have a prayer meeting for a few minutes. Some days we would be singing gospel songs all the day as we went about our work. Some mornings the text of the preacher would be chalked upon the walls or doors in the pit for everyone to read. One Christmas time, a group of us boys went to the office door (down the pit) and sang a carol. The Overman came to the door and asked if we knew what we were singing about, and then gave us a nice little address.
From Revival to Reunion by Charles H. Goodwin.

A large number of miners and their families were founder members of some of the religious institutions on Cannock Chase, such as Chadsmoor Primitive Methodist Chapel. This was built in 1876 in Moreton Street, the land purchased for £37 7s 6d. Prior to this the members met in the open air, then in their cottages before using a carpenter's shop in John Street. The miners had migrated from the diminishing Shropshire pits in their search for work, and the newly built chapel was known as 'The Shropshire Chapel'.

A Colliers' Brotherhood at Hednesford

A roving reporter for a newspaper in the early 1900s writes:

On a wet Wednesday afternoon I passed along the straggling street which dips down from Hednesford station until it comes to a full stop on Church Hill.

It is the principle street in the colliery parish. The streams of water had churned the stones up in the roadway, and scored it with many channels. There was not a soul in sight. It looked like a deserted village.

Hednesford has passed through a period of pinching poverty, and during that time many a collier and his mate have not had the wherewithal to purchase food and clothes.

As I ascended the hill I passed a man wearing a badge button on his coat. By this token I recognised in him one of a remarkable brotherhood which was initiated by the Vicar the Rev. W. Quibell three summers ago.

Up to the boom year of 1900 the coalfield had enjoyed comparative prosperity, but the following summer shortage of work made itself felt and the Vicar suggested to a dozen men in his Bible Class that they should form a brotherhood to help one another. The idea was accepted and soon there were 150 members, and at the present moment the membership stands at 500.

Each member paid 2d. a month to a benevolent fund. Distress in many cases was pitiful and the Vicar suggested that the brotherhood should lend a helping hand to their starving fellows. Sometimes only 2d. a week was left to feed a family as there was only one or two days employment, with the family living on potatoes. The shortage of labour being due to the fact that locally mined coal is household coal and little is required during the summer months.

A committee of forty was formed, and every Monday they have sat in council in the old coach house at the back of the Vicarage and listened to the cases brought in by their brethren, and doled out relief at the rate of one shilling to one and sixpence a fortnight. As they lived among the people they could judge each case fairly on its merits, and the undeserving got no sympathy, although their children were not allowed to suffer. I heard it on every side, that had it not been for the brotherhood many must have literally starved to death. Though pressed by dire need himself many a brother has given way in favour of a man with a larger family than his. This is evidence of practical Christianity from the white slaves of the Midlands.

Private persons have also generously contributed and the Vicar and Mr Albert Stanley, together with Mr Tom Coulthwaite have provided some 1500 children with one meal of bread, water and milk each day, and this was often all they had. Children have fainted away at school and men have gone to work on an empty stomach of three days standing.

The Hednesford miner is not so black in heart as his face usually is, but, taken on the whole is the very opposite of the drunken dissolute that one London writer would have us believe.

The main shopping street in Hednesford in the early 1900s looking towards Church Hill, which had rapidly expanded after the railway to Rugeley was opened in 1859. Prior to this there were a few shops at Old Hednesford, close to the Cross Keys Hotel. Most of the shopkeepers lived above their shops.

Hednesford in 1854 was 'an enclosed hamlet on the Chase', containing a number of scattered houses, 304 inhabitants and a large lake on the shore of which stood an imposing but deserted lodge built by Edmund Peel. Its main claim to fame was the 'extensive stabling for blood horses of which about 120 are generally trained in the season'.

By 1861 the population was 800, there was a railway station and the place was 'increasing rapidly'. The inhabitants were about to erect a district church, school and parsonage, the ground having already been presented by the Marquis of Anglesey. Extensive collieries were occupied by Mr Francis Piggot.

The parish church was built in 1868 and Hednesford became a civil parish in 1870. By 1871 the population was 2,229 and in 1881 it reached 7,549. The majority of the inhabitants were mining families. There were 167 mining families in 1871 and 699 in 1881. In 1871 there were 340 men employed in the coalmining industry and 1,305 men in 1881.

The Chase For Coal – The rise and progress of the Cannock Chase Coalfield 1791-1924, Charles H. Goodwin – Cannock Chase Studies No. l.

Some of the early Trustees of Chadsmoor Primitive Methodist Chapel. From left to right, back row: Charles Keeling, James Henry Haycock (miner), Ben Candlin (miner), John Titley (miner), Edward Upton (miner), Joseph Bailey (miner), Mr Humphries. Front row: Benjamin Bailey II (miner), Reuben Onions (miner), Richard Broom (miner – later grocer), Joseph Titley (miner), W. Kirkham (miner).

A group outside the Chadsmoor Primitive Methodist Chapel. From left to right, back row: John Isaac Bailey, -?-, -?-, -?-, -?-, Joseph Haycock, -?-. Second row from back: John Haycock, -?-, ? Powell, ? Titley, Isaiah Bate, -?-, -?-, Mrs Powell, Charles Keeling Snr, Charles Keeling Jnr, ? Gallear. Third row from back: Florence Haycock (with Winnie on her lap), -?-, -?-, -?-, Lucy or Eliza Darrall, -?-, Maggie Keeling, -?-, ? Bailey, Polly Burton, Polly Broom, two Upton sisters, Liza Keeling, Lizzie Haycock. Front row, sixth from left: Jessie Bailey. Ninth from left: Maude Keeling.

These families believed cleanliness was next to Godliness. They were people apart, the church was their outlet, their safety valve. In the grime and filthy conditions where they worked they found newness of life in the environment of the church.

Another Day – Another Time: A History of Chadsmoor Methodist Church, Raymond Glover.

Left: The Choir Tea at Hightown Methodist Chapel (now demolished) in 1931. From left to right, top row: Banner Carriers Albert Bailey, George Parker, Dan Middleton. Second row: George Weston, Bert Matthews, Bill Corbett, John Roberts. Third row: May Davis, Dorothy Morris, Edie Titley, Ken Roberts. Fourth row: Violet Poyser, Lottie Berrington. Fifth row: Tom Deakin, Emm Deakin, Mrs Duce, Lizzie Morris, Phoebe Titley, Bill Berrington, Jack Dunning. Seated: May Berrington, Edie Berrington, Alice Roberts and baby Garth.

Below: The Choir Tea at Hightown Methodist Chapel, 1932. From left to right, back row: Garnett Angel, Albert Bailey, Sam Bailey, Jack Edwards, Walter Horden, Cecil Stokes. Second row: Jess Turner, Dave Berrington, Ernie Jones. Harold Bullas, Jack Gretton, Dick Sirdefield, -?-, -?-, Arthur Walton John Roberts. Third row: Jean Walton, Bill Bailey, Alice Price, Tom Price, Joe Berrington, William Berrington, Ruth Berrington Lucy Matthews, baby Margaret Matthews, Joe Roberts, May Berrington, George Berrington, Tom Lowe, Tom Lane, Alf Angel, Harry Owen. Fourth row: Annie Stokes, Hilda Price, Ted Walton jnr. Mrs Joe Berrington, May Jones, Mr Jones with Rachel Berrington, Alice Roberts with Garth, Ruth Bullas with Ron, -?-, Mrs Aston, Mrs H. Owen, Mrs F. Angel, Edie Berrington, Bill Corbet, Seated: Joe Berrington, Mavis Jones, Maurice Jones.

Left: The Congregational Sunday school banner. The lady at the back on the right is Evelyn Archer.

Below: The Sunday school demonstration – this was held once a year with each Sunday school displaying individual banners, and competing with each other for the best one. The children and young people would march from their own chapel, carrying the banner at the head of the procession, to gather together in a show of strength at the front of the Anglesey Hotel, and would then progress to different locations to have tea and sports matches. It was one of the social occasions of the year and would draw a huge crowd. The top right-hand corner shows part of one of the banners and the crowd are pictured on the corner of Anglesey Street, Market Street, and Victoria Street, Hednesford.

The banner of the Primitive Methodist Sunday school at Chadsmoor. Maypole dancing was often part of the display. Note the pit chimney stack in the background.

The Our Lady of Lourdes Roman Catholic Church, Uxbridge Street, Hednesford. The building was dedicated in 1934.

St Peter's Church of England, Church Hill, Hednesford, opened in 1868. The church school and school master's house are shown in the top right-hand corner.

On the lawn in front of the Anglesey Hotel (now Anglesey Lodge), with several banners on display.

A Sunday school demonstration of the 1920s at the top end of Market Street. In the background is the old Market Hall, which was demolished in the 1960s.

Celebration tea at the Salvation Army in the late 1950s. Among those pictured are: Jack Benn, the Woodhead family, Eddie Martin, Alan Dawes, Jean, Rosemary, Keith and Mr and Mrs Watkiss, Maurice, John and Malcolm Baskeyfield, Mr and Mrs Barry Evans, Harriet, Janet, Brian and David Hunter, Cliff Calow, Polly Thomas, Gordon Wells, Miss Fowler, Mrs Harrison, the Nicholls family, Mr and Mrs Garbett.

The Salvation Army in West Hill, looking towards the station bridge, and now located in Anglesey Street, which was built as an annexe to Hednesford Technical College.

Part of the Salvation Army Band. From left to right: Mrs Gladys Martin, John Martin (son) Thomas Garbett (father and miner at 2's) Eddie Martin (miner 2's, 5's, Valley and Cannock Wood). Taken in the garden in West Hill Avenue, Hednesford.

six

Families

Above left: The 'Burgoyne Street Gang', Hightown, in the late 1920s.

Above right: Mr and Mrs S. Edwards standing in Simcox Street, Hednesford during the 1940s. The houses, now demolished, were situated behind St Peter's Church of England Junior and Infant School.

Left: Joan Barnsley and Harry Edwards in Simcox Street, 1938.

George Hendy Ball and his wife outside the coalhouse of their home in Reservoir Road, Hednesford, at the turn of the twentieth century.

Ada May and Dorothy (Ball?) outside their house in Reservoir Road, Hednesford around 1913.

Jonah and Dinah Wootton with their nine children on McGhie Street, Hednesford, *c.* 1910. From left to right, back row: Richard, Caroline, James, Harriet, Jonah. Middle row: Rebecca, Dinah Snr, Jonah Snr, Olive. Front row: Dinah, May. Jonah Snr was a first generation miner and all the children, with the exception of Olive, married miners or daughters of miners.

Dinah Wootton snr outside her caravan some time between 1911 and 1925. It was on a plot of land she purchased in 1911 in High Mount Street, Hednesford, where No. 48 now stands. At No. 50 lived Jonah Jnr and his new wife. He had the house built and it later became a general store and was later taken over by Jonah's daughter Margaret (known as Joan). She closed it in 1982 when she retired, but still continued to live there.

Left: A studio photograph of Jonah Wootton Jnr on his wedding day. He married Clara Jones on 5 June 1911 at St Peter's church, Hednesford.

Below: The wedding day of Harriet Garbett and Rex Hunter on Easter Monday just prior to the Second World War. The marriage took place at the Salvation Army in West Hill, Hednesford but this photograph was taken outside No. 46 West Hill (now Greenheath Road). The bridesmaids are, from left to right: Vera Garbett, Connie Hunter, Gladys Garbett, Annie Bishop. Back row: Jack Hunter, George Bishop, Clara Bishop, Gordon Bishop, Josiah Bennett, Harry Clayton, Ephraim Griffiths. Middle row: -?-, -?-, Mr Hunter, -?-, -?-, Gilbert Woodhead, Alice Woodhead, Eddie Martin, Les Lee, Thomas Garbett, Harriet Bennett, -?-, -?-, -?-, Louie Evans. Seated: Mrs Hunter, Mrs Garbett. The majority of the men were miners.

Wilfred Cooper (below) started work at the Valley Pit as a stallman in 1916/17, joining his elder brother and father, both named Tom. He studied to become a fireman and deputy at Cannock Mining College and passed his exams in 1941. He moved to East Cannock in the late 1950s. Around 1960 he came out of the mines with the traditional complaint of 'beat knees', as the coal seams of East Cannock pit were very low. However, mining was too deeply ingrained in his blood and he returned six months later to work at 'The Fair Lady' until its closure, and then transferred to Lea Hall, the last pit to be built and the most modern. He thought it was the most wonderful mine he had ever seen and when he retired in 1968 after nearly fifty years down the pit, he was not relieved, wishing he could have worked at Lea Hall sooner in his working life. In 1950 he was the proud owner of this 1934 Standard 9, shown here with his wife (left) and daughter. This photograph was taken in the driveway of Wilfred's home in East Cannock Road/Lower Road, Hednesford.

Wilfred Cooper in his greenhouse growing prize-winning border carnations and chrysanthemums.

Above: Miners wives Mrs Bate and Mrs Martin of Huntington Terrace Road, outside the Anderson shelter which was still in use as a coal shed in the early 1950s.

Left: Mr and Mrs Bate of Huntington Terrace Road.

Top left: Mr and Mrs Ray Martin of Huntington Terrace taken on their eightieth birthdays. Mrs Martin was the daughter of Mr and Mrs Bate.

Top right: A typical corner shop possibly kept by a miner's wife to supplement their income. The persons and location are unknown, but they are certainly local to the area. Shopkeepers were paid money by the firms who advertised on the walls of the building.

Above: Dora Thacker with Second World War evacuees Terry Joyce (left) and Billy Fleming. In the distance on the far left, the lookout post by Hednesford Hills Reservoir, used during the war, can just be seen.

Above: Dorothy Fleming, Terry Joyce (left) and Billy Fleming were from Margate and Ramsgate. Littleworth Brickworks (now demolished) can be seen in the background.

Left: Dorothy, Billy and Terry pictured at the home of Norman and Dora Thacker in Littleworth in 1940.

Out on strike, March 1912. Here the miners of Cannock Chase Colliery and their families are picking coal from the waste, to keep the homes warm and to enable them to cook.

Miners coal picking during the 1926 strike at No. 4's pit.

Local people coal picking from the pit waste mounds in Hednesford during the 1926 strike. From left to right: Mrs Perce Oliver, Mrs Clemens, Mr Harry Spiers, Mr Perce Oliver and Mr Oliver Snr.

Another group of miners coal picking during the strike. Note the wheelbarrow, sack bags and sack truck to enable them to carry away the coal. It is certain in these two photographs that the men had not been to work – they were far too clean.

During the 1926 strike all the children from Heath Hayes were fed at the church hall, and also at other places such as the Salvation Army in West Hill, Hednesford. The community rallied round to make sure the children did not starve.

Rawnsley Relief Committee during the miners strike of 1926. From left to right, back row: Tom Hackett, G. Rowley, Geo Harvey, Wesley Jones, Jos. Pinson, W.G. Bradbury, Jack Hackett. Middle row: John Cope, J.G. Taylor, John Whitehouse, William Winfindale, Arthur Share. Front row: Mrs W. Hackett, Mrs J. Hackett, Mrs J. Homer, Mrs W. Bennett, Mrs W. Harvey, Mrs J. Hall, Mrs S. Bennett, Mrs G. Joyner.

Hightown soup kitchen.

Some of these children in Chadsmoor are holdings mugs and this was probably part of the relief effort to feed miners' children during the 1926 strike.

Another group of children in the same location.

Nos 72/82 John Street, Wimblebury. These family houses were built by the colliery companies for their workers, generally very close to where they worked. Note the iron rods to the side and front of the houses – these were to try and prevent slippage due to mining subsidence.

Nos 1-13, 27-49, 55-57 Arthur Street, Wimblebury. Very typical of terraced houses built to house miners across the district. Both photographs show people sitting on their front doorsteps, a pastime that many favoured when the weather was suitable, and gave neighbours the chance to chat. Mining communities helped one another.

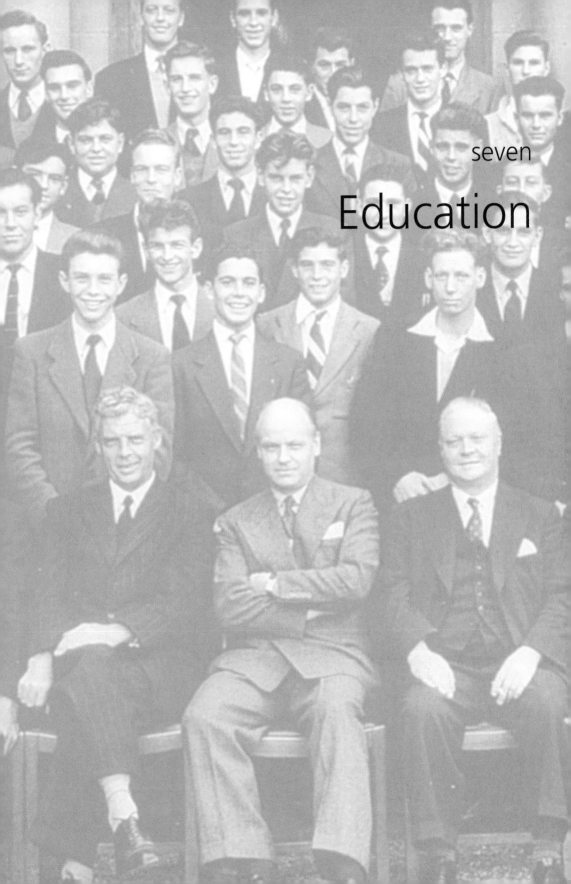

seven

Education

TELEPHONES:
DUDLEY 3471
DUDLEY 3441

TELEGRAMS:
COALBOARD, DUDLEY

NATIONAL COAL BOARD
WEST MIDLANDS DIVISION.
HIMLEY HALL,
DUDLEY.
WORCS.

BE 403A   7th. OCTOBER 1955.

Dear Mr. Spruce.

      I have pleasure in enclosing herewith
a copy of the photograph taken of the boys who
attended the third Junior Summer School this year.
Since you were one of those selected to attend,
this photograph is therefore sent to you with the
compliments of the Divisional Coal Board. I am
sure you will be glad to keep it as a reminder
of the occasion.

      Yours sincerely,

Labour Director.

Left: Typed letter to Mr Spruce included with photographs.

Below: The Junior Summer School at Keele University. In the fourth row back, far right, is Horace Spruce and directly in front of him is Jack Snape.

Union of Educational Institutions

THIS IS TO CERTIFY

HORACE SPRUCE

HAS BEEN AWARDED THIS GROUPED COURSE
CERTIFICATE HAVING SATISFIED THE EXAMINERS
IN:-

MINING DRAWING
MINING MATHEMATICS, with distinction.
MINING ENGLISH
MINING SCIENCE, with distinction.

W. E. Stevens

Chairman of the Council

H Peat

Chairman of the
Examinations Committee

J Aspinwall

Secretary

1954   16/2

Left: Certificate included with the photographs.

Below: Cannock Mining College students.
Among those pictured are Jack Snape, Dennis
Tonks, Horace Spruce, John Kendrick and
George Stephenson,

NVQ presentation to Dennis Williams (on the left) in 1997 at Coniston Hall, Chadsmoor.

Taylors Restaurant, Cannock in the 1950s. On the top table, fourth from left is Richard Payne, Principal of Cannock Mining College with, among others of his staff, Mr Reece and Mr Lejeune. Among the students were Maurice Stokes, Robert Wilkes, Horace Spruce, John Kendrick and Len Clark.

The Technical College, Anglesey Street, Hednesford (now refurbished as flats) opened on 30 September 1912 by Sir Oliver Lodge FRS, Principal of Birmingham University, at a cost of just over £3,000. It was built to accommodate mining education, but also to teach building construction and woodwork amongst others. A similar building was also constructed at Chasetown which was opened on 20 September 1913 by Professor Ashley, also of Birmingham University.

Institute of Mining, Stafford Road, Cannock. Lt-Col. W.E. Harrison and Alderman J.O. Whitehouse laid the foundation stone on Thursday 22 November 1928 and the building was opened by Viscount Chelmsford on Tuesday 22 October 1929. It was built by Messrs Green & Bird Ltd of Hednesford and funded jointly by Staffordshire Education Committee and the Miners' Welfare Fund.

Trade Union Library, Avoncroft College – Stourbridge Area.

Opened in 1931, Hednesford Park (seen here in the 1950s) was funded by the Mines Union. The site had been Hednesford Pool, shown as 27 acres on many old maps. The area had to be drained and the feeder streams piped to enable the railway line to Rugeley and the mineral line to be built.

E. Rotchell planting out the chrysanthemums.

Mr Rotchell in his greenhouse with his prize blooms.

First prize in the Annual Show at Chadsmoor.

Leisure time was used for all kinds of activities, usually combined with a supporting club, association or society. In this photograph E. Rotchell (second left) with other members, are seen inspecting garden produce at a local competition. Many miners had allotments in addition to a large garden, where they kept pigs and poultry.

Opposite below: E. Rotchell with his family enjoying a splash in the sea. Miners had the last week of July and the first week in August for their annual holiday – after nationalisation.

HEATH HAYES ALLOTTEES' AND
GARDENERS' ASSOCIATION

11th ANNUAL SHOW

SATURDAY, 20th AUGUST, 1960

FIRST PRIZE

Awarded to

MR. E ROTCHELL

Class _____2_____ Judge° _____W DODD_____

A first prize award.

SHOW COST ACCOUNT HELD SEPT. 2ND 1961

INCOME.	£ · S · D	EXPENDITURE	£ · S · D
BALANCE OF MONEY DRAWN	7 - 8 - 0	PRIZE MONEY	12 - 13 - 6
SALE OF PRODUCE.	16 - 9 - 2	REPLICA CUPS	4 - 0 - 0
RESULT OF RAFFLE.	8 - 8 - 9	TWO SPINNER AWARDS	2 - 0 - 0
SALE OF GARDEN NEWS.	1 - 0 - 0	SILVER & BRONZE MEDALS	1 - 1 - 9
SALE OF SCHEDULES	18 - 9	PRINTING SCHEDULES	3 - 4 - 0
ENTRANCE FEES.	2 - 3 - 9	PRINTING POSTERS	1 - 2 - 0
		A. KELLY. STATIONERY SUNDRIES	15 - 0
		JUDGES FEES	2 - 2 - 0
		BASKET OF FRUIT	10 - 0
		PRIZE CARDS.	18 - 6
TOTAL INCOME £36 - 8 - 5		TOTAL EXPS. £28 - 6 - 9	

INCOME AND EXPENDITURE ACCOUNT.

	£ · S · D.
TOTAL INCOME.	36 - 8 - 5
TOTAL EXPENDITURE	28 - 6 - 9
OVERHAUL PROFIT	£8 - 1 - 8

Signed:- J. T. Smith. Treasurer.
A. E. Rotchell. Sec.

Opposite above: Mr and Mrs George Woodhead outside their home with his collection of trophies, the *News of the World* cup in the centre – the top award in the UK for 1954/55 season. He also sent birds to breeders in South Africa, America and Canada, and was a show judge.

Left: A show cost account from 1961.

Below: Prize winners and their families.

Below: George Woodhead with his three champion canaries. Top centre is the *News of the World* Challenge Trophy winner and bottom left the bird which took third place in the same contest. The trophies are, from left to right: Champion Ladies Cup of Leeds Northern Roller Canary Club, the Whittingham Cup of Bilston Roller Canary Club, awarded for best two birds in show, the H. Stone Challenge Cup of Bilston RCC for best three champion birds, the United States Cup of Leeds NRCC for best faultless young bird, the Gibbons Challenge Cup of Bilston RCC, the Leeds Roller Canary Championship Challenge Cup and the P. Gray Championship Cup of Leeds NRCC.

All these cups were won during one season plus his three main successes, the *News of the World* Challenge Trophy, the Yorkshire Team Championship Cup and the Cannock Chase Roller Canary Championship Cup. His wife is shown on the right of the photograph.

George Woodhead (far left, back row), and Mrs Woodhead (extreme right, seated) with members of what is thought to be a canary breeders club. George spent all his working life in coal mining both as a miner and as a deputy, and as a result of an accident lost one eye. He was a member of the Salvation Army for many years, playing in the band and singing in the choir, as well as holding position of senior treasurer for the Hednesford Corps.

An Award Ceremony for Horace Capewell, with Les Mabberley, Len Burton, Jack Buach, Norman Leese and Bill Dunning.

Horace Capewell in front of his pigeon loft, with the Hednesford Accident Home (now demolished) extreme left in Littleworth Road.

Horace Capewell (right) receiving the *Express & Star* Cup from the newspaper representative. In the centre is a brewery representative.

Above: Albert James Wyke (better known as 'Nink') who, like many miners, kept pigeons. He worked at the pit from the age of thirteen and retired at sixty-five – fifty-two years service. He worked at 'The Fair Lady', The Coppice and latterly at West Cannock 5's and he appeared in the local press for never losing a shift at work. In his younger days he played football for Heath Hayes, and later dominoes at the Jubilee public house. The pigeon club was held at the White Lion public house in Huntington. He was eighty-nine when he died. Take particular note of his hard-working hands, but how tenderly he holds the bird.

Left: Hednesford Progressive Working Men's Club, Market Street, Hednesford.

Heath Hayes Labour Club, 1951. Among those pictured are J. Millward, A. Watkiss, L. Pugh.

West Cannock Sports and Social Club, opening in November 1957, with Harry Edwards having the first official pint. From left to right the staff are: Nobby Phillips, Colin Phillips, Barbara Miles, Dennis Phillips, –?–, Mrs Phillips. Mr and Mrs Phillips were steward and stewardess at the club.

Brindley Village Working Men's Club and Institute. A presentation to cup winners.

The 'Dicky Bow Club' at Brindley Village Working Men's Club: 'Digger' Smith, R. Bagnall, B. Baugh, R. Haywood, E. Heathcote, G. Leadbeater, L. Leadbeater

Above: The small cluster of prefabricated buildings on the Chase started life as a hospital for wounded soldiers from the First World War. Afterwards it was used by the Ministry of Pensions and in 1924 was adapted as houses for the local mining families and known as Brindley Village. In the 1950s the site was cleared and all residents were re-housed at Brindley Heath, though still retaining a strong Brindley Village identity. The village had its own primary school, church and club. Seated on the verge is Douglas Davies. Standing: Pauline Davies, Doris Garbet Olga Davies, and the Cowdell children, Russ, Doreen and Bernard. Standing behind are Mr Davies and Mr Harold Cooper. The first bungalow belonged to the Wainwrights and the second to the Davies. The dog belonged to the Wainwright family.

Right: An agreement from July 1926 between the West Cannock Colliery and the Brindley Village Working Men's Club regarding the tenancy of the club building.

AN AGREEMENT made this ___19___ day of ___July___ 1926 BETWEEN THE WEST CANNOCK COLLIERY COMPANY LIMITED (hereinafter called "The Company") whose Registered Offices are situate at Hednesford in the County of Stafford of the one part AND The Chairman, The Secretary and The Committee of the Brindley Village Working Men's Club & Institut (hereinafter called "The Tenants" of the other part which Club is registered and situate at Brindley Village in the County of Stafford. IT IS HEREBY AGREED by the parties as follows:-

(1) The Company agrees to let and the Tenants agree to take the premises known as the Brindley Village Working Men's Club & Institute.

(2) The Tenants agree to pay to the Company as rent the sum of One Shilling per annum for the use thereof.

(3) The Tenants agree to keep the premises in a good state of repair and to hand over should they at any time be required to do so to the Company in as good a condition as at the date hereof reasonable wear and tear excepted.

(4) The premises to be used as a Club and Institute and Concert Room only.

(5) The Tenants agree for the Colliery Company to have the use of the premises at any time and for any purpose should they so desire by giving to the Tenants three days notice.

(6) This Agreement to be terminated by either side giving to the other three months notice in writing to terminate at any Quarter

As Witness the hands of the parties this ___19___ day of ___July___ 1926.

On behalf of the Brindley Village Working Men's Club & Institute. *Thomas Shipman* Chairman.

Joseph Craddock Secretary.

Following page: A children's tea party in 1966 at Brindley Village WMC. Among the children are Alan Dando, Paul Mason, David Mason, Clive Mason, Paul Leadbeater, Robert Higgs.

Brindley Village Working Men's Club & Institute

BRINDLEY VILLAGE, HEDNESFORD — Registered No. 2747 Staffs. W.

Statement of Accounts for the Year ended 31st December, 1955

Dr. — Refreshments Account — Cr.

	£ s. d.	£ s. d.		£ s. d.
To Stock—1st January, 1955		168 11 5	By Refreshments, Tobacco, etc., supplied to	
„ Purchases		3012 15 1	Members	3678 5 0
„ Excise Duty	29 12 6		„ Stock—31st December, 1955	151 10 0
„ Profit to Income and Expenditure A/c.	618 16 0			
		648 8 6		
		£3829 15 0		£3829 15 0

Income and Expenditure Account

EXPENDITURE	£ s. d.	£ s. d.	INCOME	£ s. d.	£ s. d.
To Wages—Steward	301 7 0		By Profit—Refreshments A/c.		618 16 0
Secretary	39 0 0		„ Sundry Accounts—		
„ Fees — Committee	16 4 6		Subscriptions	13 0 0	
Stocktakers	18 0 0		Visitors' Fees	12 10	
Trustees	3 3 0		Interest, 3% Def. Bonds.	3 10 0	
Delegates	6 0 0				17 2 10
Help	74 19 0				635 18 10
Auditor	16 16 0		„ Loss to Balance Sheet		74 19 6
		475 9 6			
„ Rent, Rates, Taxes and Insurance		23 13 8			
„ Lighting and Heating		58 7 4			
„ Printing, Postages and Papers		12 12 10			
„ Repairs and Renewals, etc.		33 5 5			
„ Bank Charges		10 10 0			
„ Travelling		3 11 5			
„ Legal Charges		15 0			
		618 5 2			
„ Sundry Allowances	6 0 1				
„ Entertainments, etc.	12 10 4				
„ Pianist	13 5 6				
„ Refreshments to Members	27 7 3				
„ Floral Tributes	4 0 0				
„ Old Folk	1 10 0				
„ Grants, Committee	28 0 0				
		92 13 2			
		£710 18 4			£710 18 4

Balance Sheet of Funds and Effects as at 31st December, 1955

LIABILITIES & FUNDS	£ s. d.	£ s. d.	ASSETS	£ s. d.	£ s. d.
Sundry Creditors—			Stock—Refreshments A/c.		151 10 0
Refreshments A/c.	406 7 6		Furniture and Fittings, cost	1061 6 0	
Expenses	64 12 6		Less Depreciation to 1954	361 6 0	
		471 0 0			700 0 0
Coronation A/c., 1954	12 15 6		3½% Defence Bonds		100 0 0
Receipts, 1955	27 9 6		Loan		10 16 0
			Rates in advance		2 1 8
	40 5 0		Cash at Bank		2 15 0
Payments, 1955	37 10 0		„ „ „		702 6 4
		2 15 0	„ in Hand		2 10 0
Balance of Profit to 1954	1273 3 6				
Less Loss for 1955	74 19 6				
Balance forward		1198 4 0			
		£1671 19 0			£1671 19 0

Auditor's Report

TO THE MEMBERS OF THE BRINDLEY VILLAGE WORKING MEN'S CLUB & INSTITUTE

The undersigned, being an Approved Auditor appointed by H.M. Treasury, having had access to the Books and Accounts of the Club, and also drawn up the foregoing General Statement and verified the same with Accounts and Vouchers relating thereto, now signs the same as found correct, duly vouched, and in accordance with law.

Waterloo Chambers,
Cannock.
16th June, 1956

(Signed) WILLIAM BODEN
Certified Accountant and Approved Auditor under the
Industrial and Provident and Friendly Societies Acts

Statement of Accounts for the Brindley Village Working Men's Club from the year ended 31 December 1955.

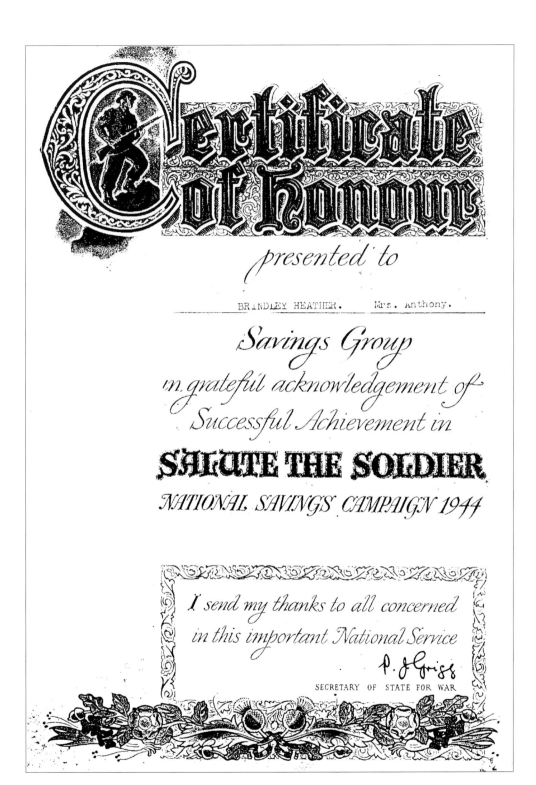

Certificate of Honour

presented to

BRINDLEY HEATHER.   Mrs. Anthony.

Savings Group

in grateful acknowledgement of
Successful Achievement in

SALUTE THE SOLDIER

NATIONAL SAVINGS CAMPAIGN 1944

I send my thanks to all concerned
in this important National Service

P. J. Grigg

SECRETARY OF STATE FOR WAR

A certificate from a savings group from Brindley Village. Schemes such as this were used to raise funds for the war effort.

'The Soldiers' attending an Old Folk's Supper in Anglesey Street, Hednesford in the late 1970s. Among the group are Jim Dowding, Mrs Dowding, Mr and Mrs Sheasby, Clara Degg and her sister, Mrs Hood and Mrs Martin. Cutting one of the cakes is Sam Morris.

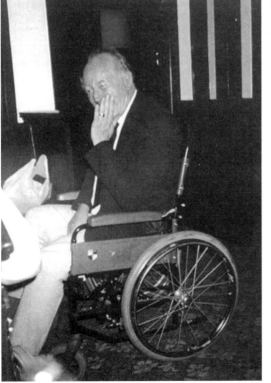

Above: Another Old Folk's Supper for the 'The Soldiers' of Anglesey Street, Hednesford, this time with bunny girl Clara Degg. Among the group are Mrs Morris and Mrs Dowding, with Sam Morris far right by the window.

Left: Bill Bott in his wheelchair, March 1998. A lunch trip for disabled miners to Hardys Pub in Oldbury. This was organised by Dennis Williams with help from the Coal Industry Social Welfare Organisation (CISWO). The CISWO was initiated by the National Coal Board in 1947. For every ton of coal produced, one penny (old money) was donated for social welfare, to enable Miners' Institutes to be founded. In the Cannock Chase Coalfield the Institutes were Lea Hall, West Cannock 5's, Hawkins and Hilton Main.

The same venue with Les Nutting in the wheelchair.

Opposite below: On 23 September 1982 a figurine was presented to Bulmer's in appreciation of a visit to the cider plant by the National Union of Mineworkers Committee. From left to right: H. Pierpoint, A. Wilkes (NUM Chairman), Bulmer's Cider Manager, their Personnel Manager and D. Williams (delegate and Cannock Chase NUM Treasurer).

Cannock Chase Mining Society at Wirksworth Quarries, 1948. Among the group are Jack Sunley (Valley), D. Jackson (Heath Hayes), Capt. C.H. Scott (Group Manager), G. Husslebee, W. Owen (Brownhills), Mr White (Group personnel), Archie Smith (Brereton), Dan Evans (Heath Hayes), Richard Jennings (West Cannock).

An outing to Blackpool illuminations in 1951. From left to right, back row: Bert Jones, Lol Anthony. Middle row: Harry Edwards, Ben Fowler. Front row: Tom Jones, Graham Brookes.

A retired miners' outing in the late 1980s. From left to right: -?-, -?-, Bill Jones, Dennis Williams, Charlie Dean, Alec Taylor, Sid Norman, Vince Anderson, Ernie ?, Bill Yapp, ? Butler, Geoff Summerfield, Harry Bagley, -?-, Harry Rowley, Bill ?, Frank Leighton, -?-, Harry Sherwood, -?-, Alan Moulter, Barry Tatler, Jim Borton.

Biddulph and Chase Retired Miners Clubs. From left to right: Maurice Galley, Vince Anderson, Jan Anderson, Joe and Rose Marriott, Joyce and Bill Colbourne, Jean Holloway, Nancy Bagley, Doreen Bott.

Hightown Women's Fellowship outing, August 1960. A large proportion of these women would be miners' wives. From left to right, back row: Nellie Ferguson, Florrie Ward, Garry Lane, David Cope, Mrs Dawson, Charlie Roadway (the coach driver) Mrs Stevens, Mrs Potts, Winnie Ridgway, Mrs Wallbank, Peggy Francis, Mrs George. Middle row: Ruby Titley, Mrs Hassall, Mrs Bisset, Mrs Slater, Hilda Bailey, Mrs Gibbons and her sister, Janet Holliss, -?-, Rose Bailey, Mrs Curral, Mrs Simister, Joyce Lane, Neville Roadway. Front row: Winnie Williams, Jessie Tomkinson, Mrs Williams, Edie Deakin, May Jones, Mrs Deakin, Mrs Morris, Dolly Marsh, Mary Broom, Maud Sanderson, Lizzie Ward.

A gala float photographer on Anglesey Street, Hednesford, now the site of the Salvation Army. The houses are no longer there. These galas were organised to raise money for the local hospitals in the days before the National Health Service.

Another gala scene. A lorry bearing the slogan 'The Toy Drum Major' and a rickshaw progressing down Market Street, Hednesford. A policeman with his cape in the foreground is keeping his eye on the celebrations.

Another scene in Anglesey Street. Note the old spelling of Hednesford.

A parade going down Market Street, Hednesford. The lorry nearest is a steam lorry and was borrowed from Cannock & Rugeley Colliery Company.

The lawn in front of the Anglesey Hotel during the carnival. In the background on the left-hand side is where the Savers store is now situated. In the bottom right-hand corner is Peter Rosa serving ice cream from his horse and cart. He was one of the first Italian ice cream vendors in the district.

A comic cricket match at Blackfords, Cannock. The only man without a hat is John Haycock and on the extreme right is Superintendant Murray. This photoraph was taken at the Central Athletic Ground some time between 1919 and 1922.

A fancy dress group, possibly near Stafford Lane. The names of the children are unknown.

A carnival float with the word 'Chadsmoor' partially obscured. Again the names are unknown.

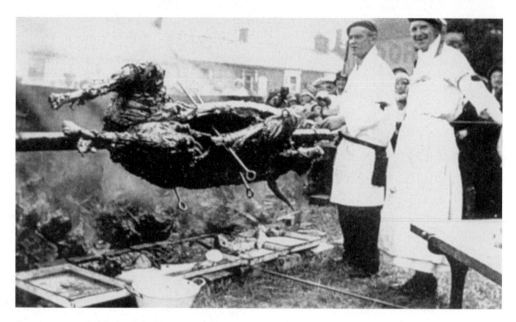

An ox roast, probably provided by one of the local butchers, on the lawn in front of the Anglesey Hotel, Hednesford. In between the heads of the two men can be seen the end wall of Moore's Clothing Factory – later the Lucas factory and later still unused.

Hightown carnival float: Bill Bailey (in the top hat), Tommy Lowe, Mr Benton, Albert Bailey, Connie and Lucy Palmer, Florrie Ward, Beattie Hindley, Doris Turner, Sally Hindley, Voilet Poyser.

nine

Retirement

THE FINAL LILYCOCK

A silent hole is all that's left
Of a world modern mans not seen,
But to many miners in retirement years
It was history not a dream,
A journey to a deep dark world
Small lights its darkness pierce,
A world of sweat and hard work toil
A battle with nature fierce,
Tiny ponies, muscles taut
As they pulled tubs along a rail,
Known by simple name and cussed
But their loyalty never failed,
Often deep in water
Marked back bent so low,
With pick and shovel the miners slave
Black diamond mounds to show,
To some it was a graveyard
As their shift did forever end,
But with loving memories they linger on
A father, a son, a friend.

Aer Reg (B.E.M.)

Opposite above: Mr Allen's farewell in the manager's office. J.D. (David) Barnes, engineer at East Cannock Colliery and photographer, compiled an album to present to Mr Allen and his wife, on his retirement. The message on the front read: 'With best wishes for Christmas and the New Year, hoping that these pictures will be of interest and some of them cause a laugh – J.D. Barnes – Christmas 1958.'

From left to right, back row: Ern Greaves, Percy Jukes, Percy Alldred, Fred Bowen. Middle row: J. Husselbee, J. Bates, Bill Guy, Charles Capewell, Mr Plant (a local preacher) Bill Parker. Front row: Harvena Williams, Mr Allen and Mrs Allen. Hanging on the wall behind is a First World War Memorial.

Opposite below: Right-hand corner: Billy Parker. Left-hand corner: A. Buttery. Centre: Harvena Williams. Note the telephone on the shelf and the underground plan on the wall.

A joke with Harvena? From left to right, standing: Mr Plant, Mrs Dangerfield, Mrs Lloyd, Sheila Yard, Wendy Lycett. Seated: Harvena Williams, Mr and Mrs Allen.

Opposite above: Horace Capewell and Pedler Palmer filling in the shaft at East Cannock Colliery prior to closure in 1957.

Opposite below: Brian Cook, blacksmith's striker, beside an old corroded fan.

Renewed steel ventilation fan driven by a steam engine made by local firm Bumsted & Chandler. From left to right: Ted Capewell, Gerald Bailey, Horace Capewell. In the mid-1950s the ventilation fan was converted to electric.

The canal basin at Hednesford, now filled in.

Above: An ariel view of East Cannock Colliery and in the middle distance the Hednesford canal basin with a row of coal trucks ready to unload the coal onto narrow boats. The fields to the left of the canal became the large Hawks Green housing estate, and the fields to the right a large industrial estate. The area covered by the pit is now also a housing estate. Just discernable in the background are the pit mounds at Leacroft Colliery.

Left: Arthur Hitchinson – charge hand fitter at East Cannock Colliery.

Above: A well-earned forty winks for Arthur Hitchinson! Note the cold tea bottle, joints for steam pipes and pump gland, keys for tool boxes, and a choice of caps!

Left: In the foreground is the canteen, at the bottom right is the Ambulance Garage and on the right-hand side is the down shaft headgear. The pitched roof behind the canteen is the electricians' and fitting shop. Behind the headgear is the Winding House, with the annex which was the mechanical and electrical engineers' office. The upcast headgear is in the background and beyond is the area of Moss Road, Chadsmoor.

Opposite below: A retirement presentation to engine winderman I. Walker of West Cannock 5's. From left to right: Errin Merret, Bert Baker, Percy Butler, Reg Langston, Isaiah Walker, Roy Walklate, Jack Jones, Joe Evans, Gilbert Bolas, Cyril Bill.

Above: East Cannock pit mound in winter. The building just visible in the bottom right-hand corner was an engine house and the two buffers are visible, with a rail running back to the colliery. The reservoir in the foreground supplied water for the boilers. The two lorries were possibly loading the spoil for filling the shaft prior to closure. The area covered by the mound is now a housing estate to the left of Stafford Lane, travelling from Hill Street. A coal truck would travel along the ridge to the top and tip spoil and cinders, many times day and night, and red-hot cinders would tumble down the sides, illuminating a dark night.

THE NATIONAL COAL BOARD CERTIFICATE

FOR LONG & MERITORIOUS SERVICE

Presented to

J. Jones

in recognition and appreciation of
68 years loyal and efficient service to
the Mining Industry and the Country

Chairman of the Board

Chairman of the Divisional Board

Above: In the canteen at West Cannock 5's in 1955 – a presentation for long service. From left to right: Fred Nicholas (Under Manager), two union officials, Tom Crellin (Manager) Bill Dando, S. Fisher, James Jones.

Left: Certificate presented to James Jones in 1955 for sixty-eight years service in the mining industry. He started work at twelve and retired at the age of eighty. After all those years as a miner, he stands as straight as a soldier on parade. A father of nine children, he lived at Fir Cottage (no longer standing) off the Brindley Heath Road, which had no running water, and kept a small holding with pigs, goats, geese, fowl and rabbits, also a large garden where he grew vegetables, fruit and flowers. He also kept watercress beds, exchanging a full handkerchief of watercress for a donation. He was also known to acquire the occasional deer! Weekends were spent drinking with fellow miners at Brindley Village Working Men's Club. He lived to a ripe old age.

A retirement function at Broomhill Albion Club in the 1960s for Mr Ball, personnel officer at Littleton Colliery. From left to right, back row: Trevor Matthews (Assistant Manager) and his wife, Carl Linney (Under Manager), W. Dolphin (Overman), Bill Simms (Deputy), George Rose, Bernard Devall, Eric Petts (Safety Engineer), Fred Phillips (Surveyor). Middle row: R. Brookes, Norman Parkin (Area Industrial Relations), Mr Barber (Manager), Bill Hickman (Under Manager), Walter Morris (Overman, NACODS Official), George Dimmock (Assistant Electrical Engineer), D. Cowley (Mechanical Engineer), Alf Powick (Under Manager), John Taylor (Electrical Engineer). Front row: Malcolm Davies, George Steed (Deputy Manager), Mrs Barber (Manager's wife who presented bouquet to Mrs Ball), Mr Ball, Colliery Nurse Sister Hession and her husband Norman.

The committee of Chase Retired Miners at Mid Cannock Club, July 1992. From left to right, back row: J. Borton, J. Marriott, H. Bagley, L. Holloway, W. Bott (Treasurer). Front row: H. Sherwood, V. Anderson, D. Williams (Secretary), C. Dean (President), E. Kerry (Chairman), W. Colbourne, W. Mair.

Presentation of miniature safety lamps to retiring officials at the Valley Colliery. From left to right: Cyril Ingle (Deputy), Jack Jennings (Under Manager), Timpy Arms (Training Officer), Clary Kelsey (Overman), Jack Boden (Deputy), Ernie Hamplett (Deputy), Will Horobin (Deputy), Jack Taylor (Overman), Jim Drinkwater (Overman). Bill Crabtree (Deputy) retired at the same time but is not in the photograph.

Above: Wrexham Miners Institute. The Chase Retired Miners Bowling Team, 1996. From left to right: Bill Colbourne, Joe Marriott, Rose Marriott, Mrs Ecclestone, Keith Bricklebank, Vince Anderson, Dennis Ecclestone, Jimmy Thompson. The prize is the Wrexham and Chase Shield.

Left: Mr G. Lee's retirement presentation from Lea Hall in 1987.

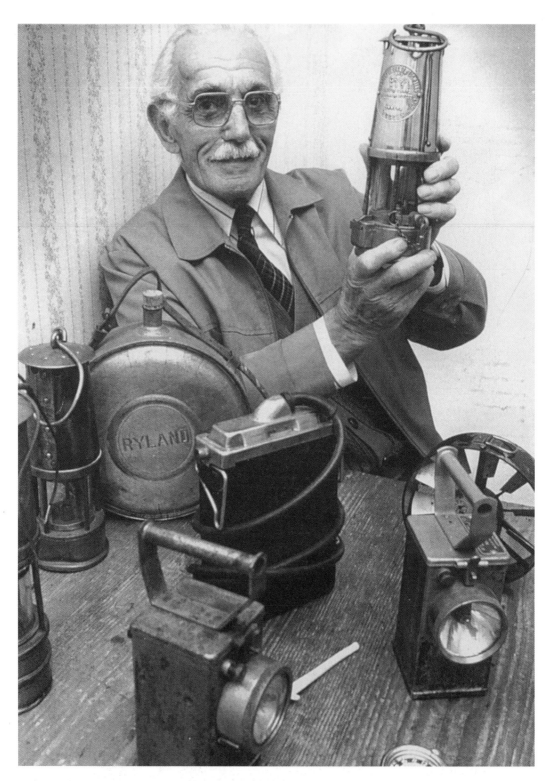

Arthur Wilkes, collector of all kinds of mining memorabilia and expert on the history of mining.

Keith Wright, a father of three children and a keen gardener, who grew all the vegetables required by his family. He worked at Cannock Chase No. 8. pit until he lost his left eye in an accident. Unable to carry on working in the pit, he delivered coal to the general public, sometimes taking his two young sons with him on his round. They returned as black as coal but with pockets full of coins the customers had given them.

A retired miner receiving his coal allowance – a very typical scene before coal was graded into size, became smokeless and was delivered in bags. Imagine the disruption to traffic if it was allowed today!

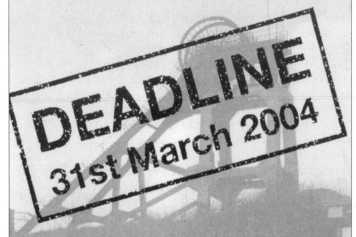

Chronic Bronchitis · Emphysema
Chronic Obstructive Airways Disease
Chronic Airways Disease
Chronic Obstructive Pulmonary Disease

DEADLINE 31st March 2004

All Current & Former Members and Widows
& Families of Deceased Members of

NUM
Midlands Area

You may be entitled to
pursue a claim for damages.

Browell
Smith & Co
SOLICITORS

The only firm of solicitors instructed
to act on behalf of the NUM (Midlands Area).

We have already recovered £125 million for the
benefit of former mineworkers and the families of
deceased mineworkers in the VWF and CBE
litigation against the DTI.

In the Cannock Chase district everything that identified with the coal mining industry has been wiped from the landscape. This leaflet is its final obituary.

THE TWO SMOKELESS BONKEYS revised 06/10/97
From the Original TWO BONKEYS (As Broadcast on
B.B.C.15.10.1977)

Two bonkeys went out one day for a stroll
To look at the pits where once drawn was coal,
To start their walk they went up to Eights
But only found stumps where once stood pit gates,
They wanted to put gypsies where once they drew coal
No more will black diamonds be pulled up this hole,
Down to the corner the Fair Lady to see
The railways now empty, on banks weeds grow free,
The slag heaps been shifted,the head gear all gone
Old man she was proud to give coal by the ton,
Down to Norton where once was the green
All that's left is a stack serene,
Where once walked the Bonkey coal tubs to move
Now stand the offices of the light industry groove,
They've flattened the pit top of poor old Jeromes
To make way for factories and new Maxim homes,
Now over the chase where stood Threes and the Fly
The sight of them gone made the poor Bonkey sigh,
We had electric from one,got tools from the other
Once owned by a family,now run by Big Brother,
They then caught a bus to see Walsall Wood
Again are more factories where once Coppice stood,
They've filled the shaft with rubbish and slush
The same shaft where coal once came with a rush,
Along Chester Road stands remains of a funny one
That went by the name of the Old Bosted Onion,
Kingswood and Cox's, Wilkin all gone
The Bonkeys were sad but with hope they walked on,
To where stood the Grove and it's disasters long gone,
Men gave their lives here in search of black gold
In Brownhills grave yard their story is told,
The pit head is gone the canal basin dead
A minute of rememberance the Bonkey bows head,
The Sinkin again has gone it's sad way
A poor old Leacroft, Mid Cannock a rubbish tip today,
What's this down at Littleton, the Bonkeys looked on
NO. Pit head wheels standing and no coal by the ton,
Where's all the horses and where is the steam
They have all been replaced chaps to keep the atmosphere clean,
They made their way home as they both began to tire
And looked at the grate saying we've still got a fire.

Aer Reg (B.E.M.)

Other local titles published by Tempus

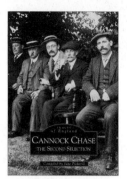

Cannock Chase The Second Selection
JUNE PICKERILL

This is the second volume of archive photographs featuring Cannock Chase. Its particular charm derives from the fact that it draws on the hidden treasure of local people's photographs and recollections. All aspects of life in the area are recalled: around the district, work, the mining industry, sport and leisure, education, transport, church and chapel and The Chase.

0 7524 1076 8

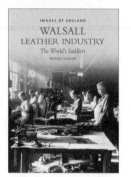

Walsall Leather Industry: The World's Saddlers
MICHAEL GLASSON

For nearly 200 years the Midlands town of Walsall has been a major centre of the leather industry, exporting saddles, bridles and a variety of horse equipment to most corners of the world. At its peak, in the Edwardian period, the industry employed over 10,000 men and women. This collection of photographs explores the history of the leather trade, which has adapted to modern times and continues to thrive.

0 7524 2793 8

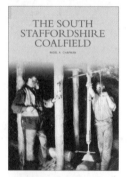

The South Staffordshire Coalfield
NIGEL CHAPMAN

At one time, South Staffordshire had the finest bed of coal that had ever been discovered. This book looks at the big four collieries – the Sandwell Park Colliery, Hamstead Colliery, Baggeridge Colliery and Hilton Main Colliery – along with the New British Iron Co. and the Cannock Chase collieries. An insight is given into the workings of the collieries and also the men who were employed there.

0 7524 3102 1

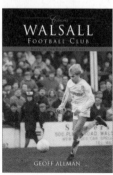

Walsall Football Club Classic Matches
GEOFF ALLMAN

What is it about Walsall Football Club that has made them far better known than most clubs who have never played in the top division or won a major trophy? The club's historian, Geoff Allman, looks at fifty of Walsall's classic games and helps fans of the club to relive the great moments of their club's history – from performing giant-killing acts against Arsenal and Manchester United in the FA Cup to winning against the odds and maintaining their Division One status.

7524 2432 7

If you are interested in purchasing other books published by Tempus, or in case you have difficulty finding any Tempus books in your local bookshop, you can also place orders directly through our website

www.tempus-publishing.com